THE BEST OF
MASTERCHEF

THE BEST OF MASTERCHEF

WITH AN INTRODUCTION BY LOYD GROSSMAN

TED SMART

A TED SMART Publication

1 3 5 7 9 10 8 6 4 2

First published in the United Kingdom in 1993 by
Ebury Press
Random House, 20 Vauxhall Bridge Road, London SW1V 2SA

Random House Australia (Pty) Limited
20 Alfred Street, Milsons Point, Sydney,
New South Wales 2061, Australia

Random House New Zealand Limited
18 Poland Road, Glenfield
Auckland 10, New Zealand

Random House South Africa (Pty) Limited PO BOX 337, Bergvlei, South Africa

Random House UK Limited Reg. No. 954009

A CIP catalogue record for this book is available from the British Library

MasterChef
A Union Pictures Production for BBC TV
Series devised by Franc Roddam
Executive Producer: Bradley Adams
Producer and Director: Richard Bryan

Editor: Janet Illsley
Design: Clive Dorman
Special Photography: Ken Field
Food Stylist: Lyn Rutherford
Photographic Stylist: Suzi Gittings

ISBN 0 09 181781 1

Typeset by Clive Dorman & Co.
Printed in Italy by Officine Grafiche De Agostini

CONTENTS

• NOTES •

Quantities are given in metric and imperial measures. Follow one set of measurements only, not a combination, because they are not interchangeable.

All spoon measures are level.

Fresh herbs are used unless otherwise stated.

Ovens must be preheated to the temperature specified in the recipe.

All recipes serve 4.

INTRODUCTION

It seems like much longer than four years ago, but it was early summer 1989 when Brad Adams, Franc Roddam and I got together for the first time to discuss Franc's idea for a new type of television cookery programme. I found the idea of 'MasterChef: The British Grand Prix for Amateur Chefs' immediately appealing. I loved the recipe which combined passionate amateurs, top professional chefs and food-loving celebrities. This, coupled with Franc and Brad's really tremendous enthusiasm and hard-headed professional skills, convinced me that the programme was going to be a huge hit. Thankfully it was. MasterChef is by far the most successful food programme ever broadcast on British television and has reached an almost institutional status with gratifying rapidity. It is now one of the regular events of the British food – and television – year.

What we have always set out to do is to be both serious and entertaining about food. Every one of us who works on the programme is committed to promoting the best in cooking, as well as to producing an enthralling and lively half-hour programme. Special mention should be made of our hard-working producer director Richard Bryan, and our production co-ordinator Melanie Jappy, herself a former contestant.

We believe that there is no place for snobbism and pretention in our red, yellow and blue kitchens: for us, good food is good fun too. Not surprisingly, a few of the great British food bores masquerading as journalists have taken us to task for insufficient piety and reverence: I must say that I pity their joyless lunches and dinners! MasterChef is a celebration of everything to do with food and we try to keep the party poopers at a safe distance.

Over the past four years we have had one hundred and eight competitors on the series. They have all cooked their hearts out and produced a succession of memorable dishes – and performances – that I would defy the amateur cooks of any other country to equal. What consistantly impresses me and everyone who works on the series is the coolness under fire of our amateurs as they industriously and beautifully cook away oblivious to lights, cameras and the probing and prodding of we lucky judges. The nerves may be there, but we and the audience rarely see them.

The trends in cooking are there too and more discernible. Our tastebuds have flirted and sometimes fallen in love with Italian, Provençal, Thai and Chinese flavours. Venison has stamped its fashionable mark, as have lavender and fresh pasta. But our contestants have always been far too good to be enslaved to any fashion and the single thread that ties them and their recipes together is 'mere' excellence. To our four MasterChefs – Joan, Sue, Vanessa and Derek – and to all our other contestants this book is most fondly and gratefully dedicated.

Loyd Grossman

STARTERS

Carrot and Coriander Soup

30 ml (2 tbsp) olive oil
1 small onion, finely chopped
1 clove garlic, crushed
450 g (1 lb) carrots, chopped
5 ml (1 tsp) crushed coriander seeds
5 ml (1 tsp) ground coriander
900 ml (1½ pints) vegetable stock
salt and freshly ground black pepper
15 ml (1 tbsp) chopped coriander leaves
coriander leaves, to garnish

Heat the olive oil in a pan and sauté the onion and garlic until softened. Add the carrots and cook gently for 10 minutes. Add the crushed coriander seeds and ground coriander and cook for a further 2 minutes. Pour in the vegetable stock, bring to the boil, then cover and simmer for 15 minutes.

Purée the soup in a food processor or blender, then season with salt and pepper to taste. Reheat if necessary. Stir in the chopped coriander and pour into warmed individual bowls. Garnish with coriander leaves to serve.

Tricia Humber

Cream of Watercress Soup

4 bunches of watercress
50 g (2 oz) butter
1 onion, finely chopped
2 cloves garlic, crushed
50 g (2 oz) plain flour
600 ml (1 pint) chicken stock
600 ml (1 pint) milk
salt and freshly ground black pepper
1.25 ml (¼ tsp) freshly grated nutmeg
juice of ½ lemon
150 ml (¼ pint) single cream

Trim the watercress, discarding the tough stalks, then chop roughly.

Melt the butter in a saucepan and gently fry the onion and garlic until soft. Reduce the heat and stir in the flour. Gradually add the stock and milk, stirring all the time. Stir in the chopped watercress, salt, pepper, nutmeg and lemon juice. Simmer gently for 5 minutes. Don't worry if it appears to separate at this point!

Purée the soup in a blender or food processor until smooth, then return to the clean pan. Reheat gently; do not allow to boil. Stir in most of the cream and adjust the seasoning.

Pour the soup into warmed individual bowls and garnish each serving with a swirl of cream. Serve immediately.

Rachel Southall

Behind the Scenes...

"Just before we began filming the first series, there was a tremendous flurry of excitement because one of the team had found some see-through glass saucepans made by an American manufacturer. They would let us film stocks, soups, etc as they were simmering or boiling away: what a breakthrough for television cookery. Alas, most of them smashed in transit from the States." ***...Loyd***

Right: *Cream of Watercress Soup*

Light Clear Fish Broth

enriched with White Wine and Peppercorns

2 leeks
2 celery sticks
½ large sweet onion
175 ml (6 fl oz) dry white wine
2 gurnard, each about 625 g (1¼ lb), filleted (bones, heads and trimmings reserved for stock)
2 egg whites
5 green peppercorns
1-2 dill sprigs

To Serve:
20 ml (4 tsp) pink peppercorns
salt
15-30 ml (1-2 tbsp) grated cucumber

Either cut the vegetables into julienne strips or roughly chop them in a food processor. Pour the wine into a pan and boil steadily to reduce by half. Add the prepared vegetables, cover and cook gently until softened.

Trim the fish fillets and cut neat diamond shapes for the garnish; set aside. Reserve all the trimmings.

Put about 1.5 litres (2½ pints) water in a large pan and add all the fish bones and trimmings, including the heads. Heat gently until almost boiling. Add the vegetables and wine, and simmer very gently for no more than 20 minutes, skimming as necessary.

Strain the liquid through a fine sieve lined with muslin into a bowl and allow to settle. Ladle out the clear broth, leaving any residue in the bottom of the bowl. (Keep the fish and vegetable mixture for clarifying the stock.)

Transfer 300 ml (½ pint) of this stock to a clean pan and heat to a simmer. Add the diamonds of fish and poach gently for 3 minutes; remove and reserve. Skim the poaching liquid and add to the strained stock.

To clarify the stock, finely chop about 15 ml (1 tbsp) of the reserved fish and vegetable mixture and mix with the egg whites. Slowly bring the stock to the boil in a large pan, whisking in the egg white mixture. Lower the heat and simmer for about 30 minutes. As the egg whites cook, they rise to the top of the pan drawing up any impurities to form a froth on the surface, and leaving the stock beneath clear and sparkling. Carefully remove the frothy layer, then ladle the soup through a muslin-lined sieve into a clean pan.

Reduce the stock by boiling to about 600 ml (1 pint). Add the green peppercorns and dill sprigs and simmer gently for 10 minutes, then strain.

To serve, add the pink peppercorns to the soup and season with salt to taste. Reheat gently, then pour into warmed soup bowls and float a diamond of fish fillet in the centre of each portion. Scatter the grated cucumber around the fish. Serve hot or chilled.

Brian Tompkins

> *"This light clear fish broth was perfection. Definitely ten out of ten."*
>
> Robert Carrier

Cook's Note

If gurnard is not available, you can use any flavoursome fish for this light broth, such as salmon trout.

Chicken Consommé

with Fresh Vegetables and Vermouth topped with Puff Pastry

60 ml (4 tbsp) dry white vermouth
600 ml (1 pint) well-flavoured hot chicken stock
125 g (4 oz) boneless chicken breast
25 g (1 oz) chicken liver pâté
25 g (1 oz) carrot
25 g (1 oz) onion
25 g (1 oz) celery
25 g (1 oz) mushrooms
15 ml (1 tbsp) unsalted butter
salt and freshly ground black pepper
400 g (14 oz) packet puff pastry
beaten egg yolk, to glaze

Divide the vermouth and hot chicken stock between 4 individual ovenproof soup tureens. Cut the chicken breast into 5 mm (¼ inch) dice. Cut the chicken liver pâté into similar dice.

Finely dice the vegetables. Melt the butter in a small sauté pan and gently sauté the vegetables in the butter for about 5 minutes until softened. Divide the sautéed vegetables, chicken and pâté evenly between the soup bowls.

Roll out the pastry thinly on a lightly floured surface and cut 4 rounds, about 15 cm (6 inches) in diameter, to fit the tops of the soup tureens as lids. Carefully position a puff pastry round on each bowl, sealing the edges with beaten egg yolk.

Brush the pastry with beaten egg yolk to glaze. Bake in a preheated oven at 220°C (425°F) mark 7 for about 18-20 minutes until the pastry is well risen and golden brown. Serve immediately.

Tony Davis

Wood Pigeon Consommé

served in a Gourd

1 wood pigeon, about 225 g (8 oz)
4 small gourds or squash

Consommé:
¼ chicken carcass (including wings, neck and legs, but not the breast, heart or liver)
125 g (4 oz) shin of beef, trimmed of fat
1 large carrot, finely chopped
1 leek, finely chopped
2 celery sticks, finely chopped
1.25 ml (¼ tsp) salt
freshly ground black pepper

Caramel:
25 g (1 oz) sugar

Vegetables:
2 white cabbage leaves
1 small courgette

To Garnish:
assorted salad leaves
snipped chives

Cut the breasts off the wood pigeon, remove the skin and set aside.

To make the consommé, break the wood pigeon and chicken carcasses into pieces and place in a large pan. Chop the beef and add to the pan together with the remaining consommé ingredients and about 1.75 litres (3 pints) cold water. Bring slowly to the boil, cover and simmer for 3 hours, skimming occasionally. Allow to cool and chill until the fat solidifies on the surface; remove the fat. Strain through a muslin-lined sieve to obtain a clear broth.

To prepare the gourds, cut a slice from the base of each one so that it will stand flat. Cut off the tops and reserve for the lids. Carefully scoop out the seeds and flesh, leaving a 2 cm (¾ inch) outer shell. Rinse the insides with hot water, drain and set aside.

Pour the consommé into a pan and bring to the boil. Cut the wood pigeon breasts into thin strips and add to the consommé. Simmer gently for 10 minutes.

Meanwhile prepare the caramel. Put the sugar in a small heavy-based pan and heat gently until dissolved, then cook for 5 minutes without stirring, until caramelised to a dark golden brown colour. Very carefully add 120 ml (4 fl oz) boiling water (the mixture will splutter) and bring to the boil, stirring, to melt the caramel. Add the caramel to the consommé to impart colour.

To prepare the vegetables, fold the cabbage leaves and cut the courgette into thin strips retaining the skin. Using a corrugated cutter, cut small decorative shapes from these vegetables. Add to the consommé and simmer for 2 minutes. Check the seasoning.

Just before serving, fill the gourds with boiling water and leave to stand for 1 minute to warm through. Arrange the salad leaves on individual serving plates. Drain the gourds and place one on each plate. Fill with the hot consommé, making sure each serving has a portion of meat strips and vegetable slivers. Sprinkle with snipped chives and replace the gourd lids. Serve at once.

Derek Johns

Mussel Soup with Saffron

and Orange

1.75 kg (4 lb) fresh mussels
2 shallots, chopped
1 leek (white part only), chopped
3 parsley sprigs
1 dill sprig
1 bay leaf
250 ml (8 fl oz) dry white wine
500 ml (16 fl oz) fish stock
250 ml (8 fl oz) water
2.5 ml (½ tsp) saffron strands
finely pared zest of 1 orange, shredded
50 g (2 oz) celery
50 g (2 oz) carrot
50 g (2 oz) leek
50 g (2 oz) butter
30 ml (2 tbsp) Noilly Prat
60-75 ml (2-3 fl oz) double cream
salt and freshly ground pepper

Scrub the mussels thoroughly in cold water and remove their beards; discard any open mussels.

Place the shallots, leek, herbs, wine, fish stock and water in a large saucepan. Add the mussels. Bring to the boil and simmer for 2 minutes. Remove from the heat and discard the bay leaf.

Lift out the mussels using a slotted spoon and remove them from their shells, discarding the shells. Set aside 16 mussels for the garnish.

Place the rest of the mussels in a blender or food processor with the cooking liquor and purée until smooth. Pass the soup through a sieve lined with a double layer of muslin into a clean saucepan. Add the saffron and simmer until reduced by a quarter, then lower the heat.

Meanwhile put the shredded orange zest into a pan with 150 ml (¼ pint) water and bring to the boil. Simmer for 1 minute, then drain and refresh with cold water. Add to the soup.

Cut the celery, leek and carrot into julienne strips. Heat 25 g (1 oz) butter in a pan, add the vegetable julienne and sweat for 2-3 minutes.

Stir the Noilly Prat and remaining butter into the soup, then add the cream and check the seasoning.

Pour the soup into warmed individual bowls and top with the reserved mussels and vegetable julienne.

Jo Eitel

Cook's Note

I had this soup in a little French restaurant in Chamonix on a skiing holiday. It came to the table boiling hot with a massive croûton which burned my tongue, but it tasted wonderful. Remember to put in plenty of garlic and ground black pepper and serve it piping hot.

Left: *Mussel Soup with Saffron*

French Onion Soup

with a croûton of Gruyère and garlic

50 g (2 oz) butter
1 kg (2 lb) onions, thinly sliced
5 ml (1 tsp) brown sugar
1.5 litres (2½ pints) pigeon, beef or lamb stock
150 ml (¼ pint) dry white wine
60 ml (4 tbsp) brandy
salt and freshly ground black pepper
2 soft bread rolls, halved, or 1small French stick, thickly sliced
175 g (6 oz) Gruyère cheese, thinly sliced
2 cloves garlic, crushed

Heat the butter in a large pan and fry the onions for 20 minutes or until very soft. Add the sugar and cook until the onions are golden brown. Add the stock and wine. Cover, bring to the boil and simmer for 1 hour. Add the brandy, and salt and pepper to taste.

Ten minutes before serving, toast the bread on one side, then turn and place the sliced cheese on the other side. Toast until bubbling and golden brown. Spoon on the crushed garlic, place the croûtons in the bowls and serve immediately.

Janet Aitken

Cauliflower and White Stilton Soup

50 g (2 oz) butter
225 g (8 oz) cauliflower florets
125 g (4 oz) onion, finely chopped
125 g (4 oz) leeks, finely chopped
125 g (4 oz) celery, finely chopped
50 g (2 oz) potatoes, finely chopped
50 g (2 oz) plain flour
1 bouquet garni (bay leaf, thyme and peppercorns)
600 ml (1 pint) vegetable stock
450 ml (¾ pint) milk
175 g (6 oz) white Stilton cheese
150 ml (¼ pint) double cream
freshly ground black pepper
30 ml (2 tbsp) yogurt
15 ml (1 tbsp) chopped parsley

Melt the butter in a large heavy-based pan. Add the cauliflower, onion, leeks, celery and potatoes, cover and sweat until transparent but not coloured. Stir in the flour and cook gently for 5 minutes.

Add the bouquet garni, stock and milk. Cover and simmer for about 30 minutes. Remove the bouquet garni.

Crumble the cheese and add to the soup, then stir in the cream. Season with pepper to taste; salt is unnecessary.

Divide between warmed soup plates and swirl in the yogurt. Sprinkle with chopped parsley and serve immediately, with toast rounds.

Juliette Forden

• Variation •

If preferred, purée the soup before adding the cheese and cream.

WARM SALAD OF WILD MUSHROOMS

WITH DEEP-FRIED POLENTA AND BALSAMIC DRESSING

Polenta:

900 ml (1½ pints) salted water
150 g (5 oz) polenta
25 g (1 oz) butter
25 g (1 oz) freshly grated Parmesan cheese
oil for deep-frying

Salad:

175 g (6 oz) young spinach leaves
1 bunch rocket leaves
22 ml (1½ tbsp) olive oil
25 g (1 oz) butter
275 g (10 oz) wild mushrooms, cleaned
1 large clove garlic, chopped
15 ml (1 tbsp) chopped flat-leaved parsley
salt and freshly ground black pepper

To Serve:

12 ml (½ tbsp) balsamic vinegar
30 ml (2 tbsp) extra-virgin olive oil
freshly shredded Parmesan cheese

First make the polenta. Bring the salted water to the boil in a pan and slowly trickle in the polenta, whisking continuously until evenly combined and smooth. Lower the heat and cook, stirring continuously with a wooden spoon, for 30-40 minutes, making sure the polenta does not stick to the base of the pan. The polenta is cooked when it leaves the sides of the pan clean.

Stir in the butter and grated Parmesan and pour into a shallow square dish. Allow to cool for about 30 minutes until set, then cut into 1 cm (½ inch) cubes.

Heat the oil in a deep-fat fryer. When it is hot, deep-fry the polenta cubes in batches until crisp and golden. Drain on kitchen paper.

Combine the spinach and rocket in a large salad bowl.

Heat the olive oil and butter in a frying pan and sauté the mushrooms and garlic over a moderate to high heat for 2-3 minutes. Remove from the heat, stir in the parsley and seasoning to taste, then spoon over the salad in the bowl.

Add the balsamic vinegar to the pan and heat, stirring to scrape up the sediment, then pour over the salad. Add the polenta cubes, drizzle with the olive oil and adjust the seasoning. Toss the salad gently and serve immediately, topped with slivers of Parmesan cheese.

Alastair Hendy

• INGREDIENTS •

Use whichever wild mushrooms are in season for this salad, such as chanterelles, hedgehog mushrooms, horn of plenty, and oyster mushrooms.

WARM GOAT'S CHEESE SALAD

WITH A WALNUT DRESSING

selection of salad leaves, eg frisée, radicchio, lamb's lettuce
2 Somerset Goat's cheeses

Dressing:

5 ml (1 tsp) light soft brown sugar
5 ml (1 tsp) Dijon mustard
1.25 ml (¼ tsp) salt
2.5 ml (½ tsp) freshly ground black pepper
135 ml (4½ fl oz) walnut oil
30 ml (2 tbsp) cider vinegar
15 ml (1 tbsp) shelled walnuts, finely chopped
15 ml (1 tbsp) chopped sage leaves

Arrange the salad leaves on individual plates. To make the dressing, in a bowl whisk together the sugar, mustard, salt, pepper and walnut oil until well blended. Add the cider vinegar and whisk again. Cover and leave in the refrigerator until required.

Meanwhile, cut each cheese in half horizontally and grill under a fairly high heat, cut side up, until melting and just golden. Arrange on the salad leaves. Add the walnuts and sage to the dressing at the last minute and drizzle over the salad to serve.

Sarah Giles

Right: *Warm Goat's Cheese Salad with a Walnut Dressing*

TRUCKLE OF WOODLAND MUSHROOMS

SCENTED WITH WHISKY

450 g (1 lb) mixed wild mushrooms
50 g (2 oz) Parma knuckle
1 clove garlic
50 g (2 oz) unsalted butter
50 ml (2 fl oz) good whisky
handful of chopped parsley
salt and freshly ground black pepper
15-30 ml (1-2 tbsp) double cream (optional)

To Serve:
warm focaccia or French bread
selection of salad leaves
vinaigrette (made with balsamic vinegar)

Trim, clean and coarsely slice the mushrooms. Roughly chop the Parma ham. Finely chop half of the garlic clove. Finely slice the other half; set aside.

Heat the butter in a large sauté pan, add the chopped garlic and cook gently until golden. Add the chopped Parma ham. Add the firm-fleshed mushroom varieties to the pan first, and sauté gently for a few minutes, then add the remaining mushrooms and sliced garlic and sauté briefly.

Increase the heat and add the whisky to the pan. Allow to bubble until all excess liquid has evaporated. Stir in a good handful of chopped parsley and add seasoning to taste. For a richer sauce, stir in the cream and heat through just before serving.

Serve on a bed of warm focaccia or French bread with a salad of seasonal leaves dressed with a little balsamic vinaigrette.

Jonathan Castle

COOK'S NOTE

Select your wild mushrooms according to the season. Use ceps, morels, hedgehog mushrooms, field mushrooms, etc. Alternatively, if wild mushrooms are unavailable, use 350 g (12 oz) button mushrooms and 25 g (1 oz) each dried ceps and morels. Soak dried mushrooms in boiling water to cover for 30 minutes. Drain and gently squeeze dry, then use as fresh ones.

• INGREDIENTS •

Parma knuckle is an inexpensive way of buying the prized ham. If unobtainable, use Parma ham or any other similar raw cured ham.

AVOCADO WITH A REDCURRANT DRESSING

3 egg yolks
salt and freshly ground black pepper
2.5 ml (½ tsp) French mustard
300 ml (½ pint) olive or walnut oil (tepid)
15 ml (1 tbsp) white wine vinegar (tepid)
125 g (4 oz) redcurrants
few drops of balsamic vinegar (optional)
2 avocados
lemon juice, for brushing

Whisk, blend or process the egg yolks, salt, pepper and mustard together until thoroughly blended. Add the tepid oil a drop at a time, continuing to whisk or blend, and increasing the flow to a steady thin stream as the mayonnaise thickens. When all the oil has been incorporated, whisk or blend in the tepid vinegar to thicken slightly.

If using a blender or food processor, add the redcurrants, and a few drops of balsamic vinegar if you wish. Blend or process until smooth, then pass through a sieve. If making the dressing by hand, sieve the redcurrants before adding them to the mayonnaise; whisk in the balsamic vinegar if using and mix well.

Halve, stone and peel the avocados. Slice each half avocado and spread out like a fan. Brush all over with lemon juice to prevent discolouration. Divide the mayonnaise between 4 serving plates and arrange the sliced avocados on top.

Peter Sayers

Right *Layered Aubergines with Tomato, Feta and Basil*

Layered Aubergines

with Tomato, Feta and Basil, and Two Sauces

4 small aubergines
salt and freshly ground black pepper
90 ml (6 tbsp) olive oil
30 g (1 oz) butter
300 g (10 oz) good ripe tomatoes, blanched, peeled, seeded and coarsely chopped
pinch of sugar
30 g (1 oz) basil leaves, finely shredded
120 g (4 oz) Greek feta cheese

Tomato Sauce:
15 g (½ oz) butter
200 g (7 oz) can chopped tomatoes
pinch of sugar

Yogurt Sauce:
150 ml (¼ pint) natural yogurt
lemon juice, to taste

To Garnish:
few small basil leaves

Cut the aubergines into 1 cm (½ inch) slices. Season with pepper. Heat the olive oil in a frying pan until smoking, then quickly fry the aubergine slices on both sides; drain on kitchen paper.

Melt the butter in a frying pan, add the tomatoes and cook for 1 minute. Add the sugar and basil and season to taste with pepper. Crumble the cheese into the pan and remove from the heat.

Layer the tomato mixture with the aubergine slices in an ovenproof dish and bake in a preheated oven at 200°C (400°F) mark 6 for 7-10 minutes.

Meanwhile, to make the tomato sauce, melt the butter in a pan, add the chopped tomatoes, seasoning and sugar. Cook until reduced by half, then strain through a fine sieve.

For the yogurt sauce, mix the yogurt with a little lemon juice to taste. Serve the terrine with the two sauces.

Vanessa Binns

RED PEPPER POTS

WITH CHEESE CORNBREAD

5 ml (1 tsp) butter
4 red peppers, cored, seeded and roughly chopped
1 clove garlic, finely sliced
pinch of thyme leaves
15 ml (1 tbsp) wine vinegar
scant 150 ml (¼ pint) double cream
salt and freshly ground black pepper

Cheese Cornbread:
175 g (6 oz) cornmeal (polenta)
100 g (4 oz) plain flour
15 ml (1 tbsp) caster sugar
10 ml (2 tsp) baking powder
pinch of salt
50 g (2 oz) butter, melted
1 egg, beaten
150 ml (5 fl oz) natural yogurt
200 ml (7 fl oz) milk
50 g (2 oz) Parmesan cheese, freshly grated
15 ml (1 tbsp) finely snipped chives
30 ml (2 tbsp) chopped parsley

"Delicious cornbread. Nice dish as a first course."

Loyd

First make the cheese cornbread. Stir together the dry ingredients in a mixing bowl, then make a well in the centre. Mix the melted butter with the egg, yogurt and milk. Pour into the dry ingredients and mix together gently, adding the cheese and herbs, to yield a thick batter.

Turn into a greased and base-lined 20 cm (8 inch) round or 18 cm (7 inch) square tin and bake in a preheated oven at 200°C (400°F) mark 6 for about 30 minutes, until risen and lightly golden. Cool on a wire rack.

To make the red pepper pots, melt the butter in a saucepan and add the peppers, garlic and thyme. Cover and cook gently for 25 minutes. Add the vinegar, increase the heat and cook until all excess moisture has evaporated. Purée the mixture in a food processor or blender, then pass through a sieve.

Whip the cream until stiff, then fold in the red pepper purée. Season with salt and pepper to taste. Divide between individual ramekins.

Slice the cheese cornbread and toast on both sides. Serve with the red pepper pots.

Orlando Murrin

Warm Chicken Liver Salad

with Smoked Bacon and Croûtons

225 g (8 oz) chicken livers
selection of small salad leaves (eg rocket, oakleaf lettuce, lamb's lettuce)
2 rashers smoked streaky bacon
2 slices white bread (a few days old)
extra-virgin olive oil, for frying

Dressing:
45 ml (3 tbsp) walnut oil
15 ml (1 tbsp) balsamic vinegar
5 ml (1 tsp) wholegrain mustard
salt and freshly ground black pepper

To Garnish:
few walnuts, roughly chopped and fried
few hard-boiled quail's eggs, shelled

Trim the chicken livers, then rinse and dry. Wash and dry the salad leaves. Cut the bacon into strips. Remove the crusts from the bread and cut into small dice. Place a 10 cm (4 inch) ring, such as a muffin ring, on each plate. Put a selection of salad leaves in the bottom and press down.

Heat a frying pan, cook the bacon strips until crisp and remove with a slotted spoon. Add a little olive oil to the pan, fry the bread cubes until golden, remove and drain on kitchen paper. If the pan looks very brown, wipe it out. Add a little more oil and fry the chicken livers for about 5 minutes. Return the bacon and croûtons to the pan and toss together briefly.

To make the dressing, put the walnut oil, vinegar, mustard and salt and pepper in a screw-topped jar with a tight-fitting lid. Shake well.

To serve, spoon the chicken liver mixture on top of the salad leaves. Spoon on a little dressing. Garnish with fried chopped walnuts and hard-boiled quail's eggs. Remove the rings and serve the salads while still warm.

Olga Morpeth

"Terribly butch"

Loyd

"This is a classic."

Simon Hopkinson

Left: *Red Pepper Pots with Cheese Cornbread*

Pan-fried Langoustines, Monkfish and Scallops

with a Spaghetti of Vegetables in Chive and Cinnamon Butter

15 g (½ oz) unsalted butter
8-12 medallions of monkfish
8-12 peeled langoustines
4-6 shelled scallops
salt and freshly ground black pepper
squeeze of lemon juice

Spaghetti of Vegetables:
2 large carrots
3 outer leaves of a fennel bulb
2 medium courgettes
1 leek
a little sugar
knob of butter

Chive Butter:
2.5 ml (½ tsp) ground cinnamon
125 g (4 oz) cold unsalted butter, diced
30 ml (2 tbsp) chopped chives

To prepare the spaghetti of vegetables, trim the ends and rounded edges off the carrots. Cut into 3 mm (⅛ inch) slices, then cut into 3 mm (⅛ inch) strips to resemble spaghetti. Place in a saucepan with a little water, a little sugar and a knob of butter. Bring to the boil and simmer for about 4 minutes until cooked but firm. Drain, refresh in cold water and drain on absorbent kitchen paper.

Repeat with the fennel and courgettes, cutting into 3 mm (⅛ inch) strips and discarding the seeds of the courgettes, but add salt to the water instead of sugar. Cook the fennel for 5-6 minutes; the courgettes for about 2 minutes. Drain, refresh and drain. Trim the leek, halve and cut into julienne strips. Cook in boiling salted water for 1 minute. Drain, refresh and drain on absorbent kitchen paper.

To make the chive butter, heat 60 ml (4 tbsp) lightly salted water and the cinnamon in a small heavy pan over gentle heat. Whisk in the cold butter a little at a time until well incorporated. Add the chopped chives.

Meanwhile cook the fish. Melt the unsalted butter in a small frying pan until hot, but do not burn. Add the monkfish and toss for 1 minute, then add the langoustines and cook for a further 1 minute. Finally add the scallops, shake the pan and cook for about 30 seconds. Season with salt and pepper. Add a dash of lemon juice. Remove from the heat.

Place the prepared vegetables in a bowl and mix carefully with a fork. Add the warm chive butter and toss well. Using a slotted spoon, lift a portion onto each warmed serving plate. Add any remaining chive butter to the fish, shaking the pan. Carefully lift out the fish and arrange around the vegetables. Drizzle the chive butter remaining in the pan over the vegetables and fish. Serve immediately.

Gregory Lewis

Cook's Note

Buy the smaller quantities of fish suggested if you wish to serve a small starter.

Behind the Scenes...

"We take great care to ensure that our enthusiastic amateurs aren't failed or former professional cooks. However we're thrilled when a successful appearance on MasterChef encourages one of them to go into cooking professionally. So far ten of our past contestants have been able to turn their passion for food into a career."

...Loyd

Right: *Pan-fried Langoustines, Monkfish and Scallops*

Nuggets of Langoustine in Basil Parcels

24 fresh langoustines
20 large basil leaves, with stems
30 ml (2 tbsp) chopped chervil leaves
600 ml (1 pint) vegetable stock

Ginger Sauce:
2 shallots, finely chopped
30 ml (2 tbsp) white wine
45 ml (3 tbsp) white wine vinegar
5 ml (1 tsp) coarsely ground black pepper
40 ml (scant 3 tbsp) double cream
250 g (9 oz) butter (preferably Jersey butter for its rich colour), in pieces
15-30 ml (1-2 tbsp) chopped fresh root ginger
salt

Salad:
4 small bunches of lamb's lettuce (corn salad)
handful of rocket leaves
handful of radicchio leaves
30 ml (2 tbsp) olive oil
1.25 ml (¼ tsp) Dijon mustard
10 ml (2 tsp) white wine vinegar
salt and freshly ground pepper

"Oh gosh, that's really delicious."

Loyd

First make the ginger sauce. Place the shallots, wine, vinegar and pepper in a saucepan. Bring to the boil and simmer until the liquid has reduced by two thirds. Gradually whisk in the cream, butter and ginger and allow to simmer very gently for 5-10 minutes. Pass the sauce through a sieve into a basin. Check seasoning and stand the basin over a pan of simmering water until ready to use.

Steam 4 whole langoustines for approximately 4 minutes, until cooked. Meanwhile peel the remaining langoustines, leaving 1 cm (½ inch) shell on the tail ends. Wash the peeled langoustines, then pat dry. Sprinkle with salt, pepper and chervil.

To prepare each nugget, lay a peeled langoustine across the width of each basil leaf. Pierce a tiny hole about 1cm (½ inch) from the tip of the leaf, wrap the leaf around the langoustine and tuck the stem end through the hole. Repeat to make 20 nuggets in total. Place the nuggets in the top of a steamer. Bring the vegetable stock to the boil in the bottom of the steamer and steam the nuggets for 3-4 minutes until the langoustines are cooked, adding the whole langoustines for the final 2 minutes to heat through.

Meanwhile prepare the salad. Combine the salad leaves. To make the dressing, place the olive oil, mustard, wine vinegar and seasoning in a screw-topped jar and shake thoroughly to combine. Toss the salad leaves in the dressing.

To serve, arrange the salad leaves on individual plates. Position the langoustine nuggets in a circle on each plate and spoon over some of the ginger sauce. Place a whole langoustine in the centre of each circle. Serve immediately, accompanied by the remaining sauce.

Jo Eitel

Mussels in Mildly Spiced Coconut Sauce

1.75 kg (4 lb) mussels
65 g (2½ oz) unsalted butter
175 g (6 oz) shallots, finely chopped
2 cloves garlic, crushed
2.5 cm (1 inch) piece fresh root ginger, grated
1.25 ml (¼ tsp) turmeric
5 ml (1 tsp) ground cumin
250 ml (8 fl oz) coconut milk (fresh or canned)
250 ml (8 fl oz) chicken stock
salt and freshly ground pepper
15 ml (1 tbsp) chopped coriander leaves

Cook's Note

I normally use fresh coconut milk, although you can use the canned variety for convenience. To make fresh coconut milk: fill a measuring jug to 450 ml (¾ pint) with grated fresh coconut, then put into a food processor or blender. Add 300 ml (½ pint) very hot water and blend for a few seconds. Line a sieve with muslin and place over a bowl. Empty the contents into the sieve. Gather the corners of the muslin and squeeze out the liquid.

Scrub the mussels thoroughly in cold water, discarding any that are damaged or open.

Heat 15 ml (1 tbsp) butter in a pan, and fry the shallots until they become translucent. Add the garlic, ginger, turmeric and cumin and fry over moderate heat, stirring continuously, for 5 minutes to thoroughly cook the spices. Add the coconut milk, stock and seasoning. Bring to the boil, then simmer until the sauce has reduced by a third.

"Can I have another one?"

Sophie Grigson

Strain the sauce into a large pan. Add the mussels, cover and cook over moderate heat for 4 minutes or until the shells open; discard any unopened mussels. Remove the mussels from the sauce with a slotted spoon and keep warm.

Strain the sauce and reduce over a high heat until it becomes slightly syrupy. Remove from the heat, then whisk in the remaining butter in pieces, a little at a time.

Remove the empty upper shell from each mussel and put the mussels into warmed soup bowls. Pour the desired amount of sauce over the mussels and sprinkle with coriander to serve.

Amita Baldock

Mussels with Pistou

1 kg (2 lb) mussels
150 ml (¼ pint) dry white wine
3 cloves garlic
10 very fresh basil sprigs
30-45 ml (2-3 tbsp) olive oil
salt and freshly ground black pepper
rock salt, to serve (optional)

Cook's Note

Pistou is a classic Provençal mix which you can use in soups and pastas, providing you like garlic! The garlic, basil and oil must be ground in a pestle and mortar. Although this is a lengthy process it really makes a difference to the end result.

Scrub the mussels thoroughly under cold water, removing their beards and discarding any opened ones. Put the mussels in a pan with the wine and cover with a tight-fitting lid. Place over a moderate heat until the shells have opened; discard any unopened ones. Drain the mussels and remove the empty half shells.

In a mortar, pound the garlic and basil until smooth. Add the olive oil drop by drop until the mixture forms a smooth paste. Season to taste with salt and pepper Add a little pistou to each half mussel and heat briefly under a hot grill.

Set the mussels on a layer of rock salt to serve, if you wish.

Joan Bunting

"Rustic, straightforward and honest"

Anton Mosimann

Oysters with Raspberry Sauce

16 oysters
25 g (1 oz) shallots, finely chopped
50 g (2 oz) unsalted butter
15 ml (1 tbsp) raspberry vinegar
15 ml (1 tbsp) raspberry purée
30 ml (2 tbsp) double cream
30 ml (2 tbsp) medium dry white wine
salt and freshly ground white pepper
50 g (2 oz) fine French beans
25 g (1 oz) mushrooms, finely chopped

To Garnish:
coarse sea salt
raspberries

"It's absolutely stunning... awfully good."

Derek Nimmo

Open the oysters over a bowl to collect the juice. Lay the oysters on kitchen paper and set aside. Strain the juice.

Gently fry the shallots in a little of the butter until soft, but not coloured. Add the oyster juice, vinegar and raspberry purée. Cook over a high heat until reduced and syrupy. Add the cream and wine. Let the sauce bubble briefly, then remove from the heat and beat in the rest of the butter, a little at a time. Adjust the seasoning.

Cut the French beans into 1 cm (½ inch) lengths and boil until tender but still crisp; drain. Refresh under cold water, drain and cut into julienne. Set aside half of the beans for garnish; add the rest to the sauce.

Boil the empty deeper halves of the oyster shells to clean and warm them. Set the shells on warmed plates lined with sea salt.

Add the chopped mushrooms and oysters to the sauce and place over a medium heat. As soon as the sauce starts to tremble, spoon into the oyster shells. Garnish with the julienne of French beans and raspberries to serve.

Amita Baldock

Oysters au Gratin

12 oysters, scrubbed clean
100 ml (3½ fl oz) dry white wine
1 carrot, sliced
1 stick celery, sliced
15 ml (1 tbsp) lemon juice
100 ml (3½ fl oz) single cream
2 egg yolks
salt and freshly ground black pepper
30 ml (2 tbsp) grated mozzarella cheese

To Serve:
45 ml (3 tbsp) rock salt
lemon wedges
herb sprigs

"The oysters gave a great tang of the sea the moment you took a taste. It was terrific."

Martyn Lewis

Right: *Oysters au Gratin*

Put the oysters on a baking tray and place in a preheated oven at 180°C (350°F) mark 4 for 1-2 minutes until they open. Remove the oysters from their shells, reserving the juices. Clean out the empty shells.

Place the white wine, carrot, celery, lemon juice and reserved oyster juice in a saucepan and cook for 5 minutes until the vegetables are tender and the stock is reduced. Strain the stock, discarding the vegetables (they are simply used to add flavour).

Return the oysters to their shells and place in a baking dish. In a bowl, whisk the cream and egg yolks together, then pour on the stock, stirring. Return to the pan and cook gently over a low heat, stirring constantly, until slightly thickened. Season with salt and pepper to taste, then pour the sauce evenly over the oysters.

Sprinkle with the grated cheese and place under a preheated grill until melted and lightly browned. Serve the oysters, three per person, each resting on a bed of rock salt. Garnish with lemon wedges and herb sprigs.

Betsy Anderson

Crab and Ginger Wontons

with a Citrus Sauce

12 wonton skins

Filling:

75 g (3 oz) Dover sole fillet, skinned
1 egg
60 ml (2 fl oz) double cream
175 g (6 oz) white crabmeat
7.5 ml (1½ tsp) grated fresh root ginger
7.5 ml (1½ tsp) light soy sauce
5 ml (1 tsp) rice wine
15 ml (1 tbsp) finely chopped coriander leaves
2.5 ml (½ tsp) sugar
salt and freshly ground pepper

Citrus Sauce:

300 ml (½ pint) fish stock
1 pink grapefruit, peeled and segmented
juice of 1 lemon
1.25 ml (¼ tsp) Dijon mustard
2 thin slices fresh root ginger
30 ml (2 tbsp) double cream
50 g (2 oz) unsalted butter, chilled

To Garnish:

tomato concassé (see note)
coriander leaves

Place the Dover sole, egg and cream in a food processor or blender and process for about 1 minute. Transfer to a bowl, add the remaining filling ingredients and mix thoroughly by hand. Check the seasoning.

Place a generous spoonful of the filling in the middle of each wonton skin. Bring up the sides of the wonton skin and press them down over the top of the filling. Tap the wonton on the bottom to make a flat base. The top should be wide open, exposing the filling. Put the wontons on a heatproof plate and cook in a steamer for 20-25 minutes.

Meanwhile, make the citrus sauce. Bring the fish stock to the boil, then add the grapefruit segments, lemon juice, mustard and ginger. Boil the sauce until it has reduced and the grapefruit segments have broken up. Press through a sieve, then add the double cream. Whisk in the butter, a little at a time, over a low heat. Adjust the seasoning.

To serve, pour a pool of sauce on to each serving plate. Position 3 wontons on each pool of sauce, with a little tomato concassé in the centre. Scatter coriander leaves between the wontons. Serve immediately.

Amita Baldock

• Ingredients •

Wonton skins are available fresh or frozen from Oriental food stores and supermarkets. They are approximately 7.5 cm (3 inches) square.

Cook's Note

For the tomato concassé, simply peel and seed a few tomatoes, then finely chop the flesh.

Maryland Crabcakes

with Tartare Sauce

Crab Cakes:

1 large egg
22 ml (1½ tbsp) double cream
7.5 ml (1½ tsp) Dijon mustard
2.5 ml (½ tsp) Worcestershire sauce
5 ml (1 tsp) Old Bay seasoning
pinch of cayenne pepper
freshly ground pepper
22 ml (1½ tbsp) minced spring onions
15 ml (1 tbsp) minced fresh parsley
60 ml (4 tbsp) mayonnaise
450 g (1 lb) crabmeat
22 ml (1½ tbsp) ground almonds
50 g (2 oz) fine breadcrumbs
225 g (8 oz) clarified butter

Tartare Sauce:

15 ml (1 tbsp) Champagne vinegar
7.5 ml (1½ tsp) Dijon mustard
pinch of salt
freshly ground pepper
Tabasco sauce to taste
125 ml (4 fl oz) mayonnaise
½ medium onion, finely chopped
30 ml (2 tbsp) finely chopped dill pickles
30 ml (2 tbsp) finely chopped parsley
7.5 ml (1½ tsp) finely chopped chives
15 ml (1 tbsp) chopped capers

To Garnish:

60 ml (4 tbsp) finely chopped parsley

Right: *Maryland Crabcakes with Tartare Sauce*

To make the crab cakes, lightly whisk the egg in a large mixing bowl, then add the cream, mustard, Worcestershire sauce, Old Bay seasoning, cayenne and pepper to taste, and continue whisking until well blended. Add the spring onions, minced parsley and mayonnaise and mix until all of the ingredients are well blended. Gently fold in the crabmeat and ground almonds, taking care to break up the crabmeat as little as possible.

Using the hands, form the mixture into 4 equal-sized cakes and coat each cake lightly with breadcrumbs. Place the crab cakes on a baking sheet, cover and chill for 1 hour.

Meanwhile, make the tartare sauce. Put the vinegar, mustard, salt, pepper and Tabasco in a bowl and whisk until well blended. Add the mayonnaise, onion, pickles, parsley, chives and capers, and beat thoroughly until the ingredients are well blended. Cover and chill until required.

Heat the clarified butter in a large, heavy-based frying pan over a moderate heat. Add the crabcakes and fry for 3-4 minutes on each side until golden brown. Drain on absorbent kitchen paper and keep warm. Sprinkle each cake with chopped parsley and serve accompanied by the tartare sauce and a green salad.

Martha Spencer

Buckwheat Pancakes with Smoked Salmon

and Horseradish Cream

Pancakes:
150 ml (¼ pint) milk
75 ml (5 tbsp) water
2.5 ml (½ tsp) caster sugar
15 g (½ oz) butter
125 g (4 oz) plain flour
50 g (2 oz) buckwheat flour
1.25 ml (¼ tsp) salt
1 egg, separated
butter or oil, for frying

Topping:
50-75 g (2-3 oz) piece smoked salmon fillet, diagonally sliced
5-10 ml (1-2 tsp) freshly grated horseradish (or creamed horseradish)
150 ml (¼ pint) soured cream

To Garnish:
snipped chives

To make the pancakes, put the milk, water, sugar and butter in a saucepan and heat gently until melted. Pour into a food processor and add the plain and buckwheat flours, salt and egg yolk. Blend to a smooth batter. Transfer to a bowl, cover and leave in a warm place for 1-1½ hours until frothy. Whisk the egg white until soft peaks form and fold into the batter.

To cook the pancakes, heat a griddle or heavy-based frying pan until very hot. Grease with butter or oil and drop dessertspoonfuls of batter into the pan, spacing well apart. Cook for 1-2 minutes, then place a piece of smoked salmon in the centre of each one. Flip over and cook until the underside is golden brown. Wrap the pancakes loosely in a greased foil parcel and keep warm in a low oven, while cooking the remainder.

Mix the horseradish with the soured cream and serve as a topping for the pancakes. Garnish with chives. Serve immediately.

Sue Lawrence

Cook's Note

Ideally you need a piece of smoked salmon which you can slice obliquely (rather than pre-packed thin slices) for these pancakes.

Skate Wing

with a Soy Vinaigrette and Salad

575 g (1¼ lb) skate wing
65 g (2½ oz) butter, melted
30 ml (2 tbsp) soy sauce
5-10 ml (1-2 tsp) chopped tarragon
½ leek (white part only)
½ stick celery
1 carrot
1 courgette
salt and freshly ground black pepper
2 shallots, finely chopped
300 ml (½ pint) fish stock
15 ml (1 tbsp) oil
15 ml (1 tbsp) tarragon vinegar
1 bunch of chives, snipped

Salad:
100 g (3½ oz) young spinach leaves
100 g (3½ oz) rocket
175 g (6 oz) frisée
2 tomatoes, skinned, seeded and diced

"This is the sort of first course everyone likes – light and clean."

Loyd

Place the skate on a large piece of foil. Flavour 50 g (2 oz) of the butter with a little of the soy sauce and chopped tarragon and brush over the fish. Cut the leek, celery, carrot and courgette into julienne strips and sprinkle over the fish. Season with salt and pepper. Wrap tightly to form a parcel, sealing the edges well. Place in the top of a steamer and steam for 5 minutes or until the fish is cooked. Meanwhile sweat the shallots in the remaining butter until softened.

Skin and fillet the skate, reserving the cooking juices and vegetable julienne, keep warm. Pour the fish stock and cooking juices into a pan, bring to the boil and reduce by half, then strain.

Whisk together the oil, vinegar and remaining tarragon, then whisk 15 ml (1 tbsp) of this dressing into the sauce to enrich it. Add half of the shallots, chives and remaining soy sauce to the sauce. And the other half of these ingredients to the dressing.

Arrange the salad leaves around the edge of the serving plates and brush with the dressing. Place the skate fillets in the centre, spoon on the sauce and sprinkle with the vegetable julienne and diced tomatoes. Serve immediately.

Helen Weller

Salmon Tartare

with Crème Fraîche and Dill Vinaigrette

225 g (8 oz) skinned salmon fillets
125 g (4 oz) gravad lax
125 g (4 oz) clarified butter
1 shallot, finely diced
1 clove garlic, halved
5 ml (1 tsp) chopped dill
lemon juice, to taste
salt and freshly ground black pepper

Dill Vinaigrette:
60 ml (4 tbsp) olive oil
15 ml (1 tbsp) white wine vinegar
2.5 ml (½ tsp) chopped dill
30 ml (2 tbsp) finely diced tomato flesh

To Serve:
60 ml (4 tbsp) crème fraîche

Finely dice the salmon and gravad lax and mix well.

Heat the clarified butter in a pan and sauté the shallot and garlic for 1 minute, then discard the garlic. Add the butter mixture to the salmon together with the dill and lemon juice to taste. Season with salt and pepper to taste. Mix well and chill in the refrigerator until required.

Whisk together the ingredients for the vinaigrette, or shake vigorously in a screw-topped jar, adding salt and pepper to taste.

To serve, spoon the dill vinaigrette on to individual serving plates. Form the salmon tartare into quenelles, using two moistened tablespoons to shape the ovals. Position 3 quenelles on each plate and spoon some crème fraîche into the middle. Serve at once.

Michael Baxter

Cook's Note

Gravad Lax is lightly salted salmon flavoured with dill; a Swedish speciality, it is widely available in this country. You will find it easier to dice and mix the fish if it is partially frozen first.

• Ingredients •

Clarified butter can be heated to a much higher temperature than ordinary butter without burning. To prepare clarified butter, melt the butter in a pan over a low heat, then skim the froth from the surface. Remove from the heat and allow to stand until the sediment settles on the base of the pan. Carefully pour the clarified butter into a clean bowl, leaving the sediment behind.

Arbroath Smokie Mousse

with Shredded Vegetables and Vinaigrette

1 large Arbroath smokie, skinned and filleted, 300 g (10 oz) filleted weight
2 eggs
salt and freshly ground black pepper
200 ml (7 fl oz) double or soured cream

Shredded Vegetables:
1 carrot
1 courgette
1 small cooked beetroot

Vinaigrette:
7.5 ml (1½ tsp) Dijon mustard
22 ml (1½ tbsp) oil (preferably white truffle oil)
7.5 ml (1½ tsp) white wine vinegar

Base:
100 g (4 oz) cabbage, finely shredded
25 g (1 oz) butter
25 g (1 oz) pine nuts, toasted

Purée the fish in a blender or food processor with the eggs and salt and pepper. Transfer to a bowl, cover and chill in the refrigerator for 1 hour.

Butter 4 individual moulds, each about 120 ml (4 fl oz) capacity. Line a bain-marie (or roasting tin) with greaseproof paper.

Gradually incorporate the cream into the fish mixture, then pass the mixture through a food mill to remove any bones. Spoon the smokie mixture into the moulds and place in the bain-marie; the hot water should come halfway up the sides of the moulds. Cover with a sheet of foil that has been pierced in a few places. Cook in a preheated oven at 160°C (325°F) mark 3 for about 20-30 minutes until set.

Meanwhile, finely grate the carrot, courgette and beetroot, keeping them separate. Combine the ingredients for the vinaigrette and season with salt and pepper to taste.

Just before serving, sauté the cabbage in the butter until crisp and tender. Add the pine nuts; do not overcook the cabbage.

To serve, place a little of the cabbage in the centre of each warmed serving plate and unmould the mousses on top of the cabbage. Decorate with the shredded vegetables, arranging them one on top of another. Warm the vinaigrette, then pour around the vegetables. Serve immediately.

Martha Spencer

Cook's Note

If you are filleting the fish yourself, first warm it slightly in the oven as this enables the flesh to be removed more easily.

Millefeuilles of Salmon and Savoy Cabbage

with a Sabayon of Sherry

1 medium Savoy cabbage
salt and freshly ground black pepper
12 cm (5 inch) piece of salmon tail, about 225 g (8 oz)
125 g (4 oz) butter, melted
250 ml (8 fl oz) dry white wine
lemon juice, to taste

Sabayon Sauce:
2 egg yolks
15 ml (1 tbsp) dry sherry

Remove the 4 outer leaves from the cabbage and discard. Carefully remove the next 16 leaves, cutting through the stalks at the base and peeling off without tearing. Wash leaves and pat dry with kitchen paper.

Using a 6 cm (2½ inch) pastry cutter, carefully cut out a round from each leaf. Reserve the rest of the cabbage. Add the cabbage rounds to a pan of boiling salted water and boil for 8 minutes. Drain and pat dry with kitchen paper. Put the leaves on a plate, cover and leave in the refrigerator for 10 minutes to firm up.

Meanwhile, prepare the salmon. Remove the skin and bones, then slice the flesh as thinly as possible.

Finely shred half of the remaining cabbage leaves, discarding the centre ribs. Put the shredded cabbage in a pan with 75 g (3 oz) of the melted butter and cook, stirring, for 2 minutes. Add the white wine and cook gently for 10 minutes.

Remove from the heat and leave until cold, then press the mixture in a fine sieve over a bowl squeezing to extract the cabbage juices; reserve for the sauce. Keep the shredded cabbage for the millefeuilles filling.

To prepare the millefeuilles, set aside four dark green cabbage rounds for the top layer. To assemble each millefeuilles, brush a cabbage round with a little melted butter, cover with a fine layer of salmon, then add a squeeze of lemon juice and salt and pepper. Add a thin layer of cold shredded cabbage. Repeat these layers twice, then cover with a reserved dark green cabbage round, leaving the top cabbage round unbuttered. Assemble another 3 millefeuilles, in the same way.

To make the Sabayon sauce, put the egg yolks, sherry and 15 ml (1 tbsp) water in the top of a double boiler or in a heatproof bowl over a pan of hot water placed over a medium heat. Whisk constantly until the mixture thickens. Reheat the reserved cabbage juices and whisk into the sabayon, a little at a time. Season with salt and pepper to taste and keep warm.

Place the 4 millefeuilles in a steamer basket over a pan of boiling water and steam for 8 minutes. Carefully transfer to warmed serving plates and spoon on the sabayon sauce. Serve immediately.

Derek Johns

Salmon and Asparagus Mousse

225 g (8 oz) salmon fillets
2 eggs, plus 2 egg yolks
150 ml (¼ pint) double cream
salt and freshly ground black pepper
1 bundle of asparagus
125 g (4 oz) unsalted butter
finely grated rind and juice of ½ lemon

Cook's Note

The lemon sauce accompanying this mousse is a cheeky way of making hollandaise sauce and it's foolproof!

Purée the salmon in a food processor until smooth. Add 1 egg, the cream, and salt and pepper to taste. Process briefly until evenly combined. Allow to cool, and chill.

Meanwhile, steam the asparagus or cook in boiling salted water until tender; drain thoroughly. Reserve some of the tips as a garnish. Purée the remaining asparagus in the food processor, add 1 egg and season with salt and pepper. Process briefly until evenly combined. Allow to cool, and chill.

Butter 4 dariole moulds or ramekins and divide half the salmon mixture between them; each mould should be one-third filled. Add a layer of asparagus mousse and top with the remaining salmon mousse. Cover with buttered greaseproof paper and place in a shallow baking tray half-filled with water. Cook in a preheated oven at 190°C (375°F) mark 5 for 25 minutes or until firm.

To make the sauce, melt the butter with the lemon rind, and season with salt and pepper. Blend the egg yolks and lemon juice in a food processor or blender then, with the motor running, add the hot butter in a steady stream until blended. Turn each mousse out on to a warmed serving plate and pour around some of the lemon sauce. Garnish with the asparagus tips and serve immediately.

Joan Bunting

Derek Johns – Winner 1993

From Devizes in Wiltshire, Derek Johns is the latest holder of the coverted MasterChef title and the first male winner. As a fine art dealer with a gallery in St James', Derek travels the world uncovering and restoring period paintings. At home, he is an enthusiastic gardener as well as a brilliant cook.

"*A marriage made in heaven.*"

Pierre Koffmann

Hot Smoked Wild Salmon Sauce

on a Green Salad

50 g ($1\frac{3}{4}$ oz) can anchovies in oil
300 ml ($\frac{1}{2}$ pint) double cream
5 ml (1 tsp) tomato purée
freshly ground black pepper
a little finely chopped parsley
125 g (4 oz) smoked wild salmon, cut into ribbons

Below: *Hot Smoked Wild Salmon Sauce on a Green Salad*

Salad:
assorted salad leaves 'with bite', eg chicory, watercress, frisée
few spring onions
handful of mangetout, finely sliced
few tarragon leaves
lime juice, to taste
small handful each of green and pink peppercorns in brine, drained

Drain the anchovies, reserving the oil. Place half of them in a heavy-based saucepan with the anchovy oil. Cook over a low heat, stirring with a wooden spoon, to make a smooth paste. Add the cream and tomato purée, stirring until the mixture bubbles. Continue cooking over a low heat, stirring occasionally, until a thick sauce is formed.

Add pepper to taste and a tiny amount of finely chopped parsley. Set aside a few of the smoked salmon ribbons for garnish; add the rest to the sauce.

Combine the salad leaves, spring onions, mangetout and tarragon leaves in a bowl. Sprinkle with lime juice and pepper to taste. Arrange the salad in individual bowls and dot with green and pink peppercorns. Sprinkle with the reserved ribbons of salmon.

Pour the hot sauce over the salad and serve immediately.

Linda Yewdall

Chicken Livers with Salsa

125 g (4 oz) chicken livers
4 shallots
30 ml (2 tbsp) olive oil
50 g (2 oz) oyster mushrooms

Marinade:
125 ml (4 fl oz) sherry
2 cloves garlic, crushed
4 black peppercorns
salt and freshly ground pepper
handful of chopped basil
10 ml (2 tsp) sesame oil

Salsa:
1 red pepper
½ green pepper
2 small red chillis (or to taste)
2 shallots
15 ml (1 tbsp) capers
15-30 ml (1-2 tbsp) olive oil
15 ml (1 tbsp) white wine vinegar
juice of ½ lime
salt and freshly ground pepper

To Serve:
rocket leaves

Combine all the ingredients for the marinade in a shallow dish. Add the chicken livers and leave to marinate for 3-4 hours or overnight if possible. Drain the livers, then cut into strips.

To make the salsa, remove the core and seeds from the peppers and chillis. Chop the peppers, chillis, shallots and capers very finely. Place in a small bowl. Add the olive oil, vinegar, lime juice and seasoning, mix well and leave to stand.

Cut the shallots into bite-sized pieces. Heat 15 ml (1 tbsp) olive oil in a pan and cook the shallots gently for a few minutes. Add the sugar and cook until the shallots are soft and caramelised. Set aside.

Heat the remaining olive oil in the clean pan and sauté the chicken livers for 2-3 minutes. Add the mushrooms and cook for a further 30 seconds. Remove with a slotted spoon and mix with the caramelised shallots. Add the rocket leaves and toss very gently. Serve immediately, with the salsa.

Melanie Jappy

Goat's Cheese and Cherry Parcels

4 small round English goat's cheeses
20 ml (4 tsp) kirsch
4 sheets filo pastry
about 60 ml (4 tbsp) melted unsalted butter
40 ml (8 tsp) stoned Morello cherries, juice reserved
20 ml (4 tsp) sesame seeds
60 ml (4 tbsp) grapeseed oil
15 ml (1 tbsp) cherry juice
squeeze of lime juice
salt and freshly ground black pepper
assorted salad leaves, to serve
Morello cherries, to garnish

De-rind the goat's cheeses, sprinkle each one with 5 ml (1 tsp) kirsch and set aside for at least 1 hour. Take 1 sheet of filo pastry and brush with melted butter. Fold in half and cut out as large a circle as possible. Brush with butter. Place a goat's cheese in the centre of the filo and put about 10 ml (2 tsp) cherries on top of the cheese. Gather the filo pastry over the cherries and pinch together to form a parcel. Brush with butter and sprinkle with 5 ml (1 tsp) sesame seeds. Repeat to make 4 parcels in total.

Place the filo parcels on a greased baking tray and bake in a preheated oven at 200°C (400°F) mark 6, for 10-15 minutes until golden. Meanwhile, put the oil, cherry juice, lime juice and salt and pepper in a screw-topped jar and shake well. Toss the salad leaves with the dressing.

Serve the parcels very hot on individual plates with the salad. Garnish with a few cherries.

Joan Bunting

Behind the Scenes...

"Our contestant kitchens sit on a solid concrete studio floor with no service runs and have to be completely self-contained. Clean water is stored in one tank and waste water in another: minor floods have happened! Each kitchen has its own cylinder of North Sea gas which is replaced for every show and as a result a team of gas engineers in their distinctive blue overalls is an intregal part of the studio team."

...Loyd

PAN-FRIED DUCK BREAST

ON A SALAD OF BRAISED RED CABBAGE

2.5 ml (½ tsp) salt
2 large duck breasts, each weighing 275 g (10 oz)
4 handfuls of mixed salad leaves, eg radicchio, curly endive, lamb's lettuce, sorrel

Braised Red Cabbage:
30 ml (2 tbsp) olive oil
1 large onion, chopped
1 small red cabbage, cored and finely sliced
1 large cooking apple
15 ml (1 tbsp) brown sugar
60 ml (4 tbsp) red wine vinegar (approximately)
2.5 ml (½ tsp) caraway seeds
1 bay leaf
4 allspice berries, crushed
salt and freshly ground black pepper

Orange Dressing:
1 orange
5 ml (1 tsp) white wine vinegar
5 ml (1 tsp) Dijon mustard
salt and freshly ground black pepper
15-25 ml (3-5 tsp) olive oil

To Serve:
15 ml (1 tbsp) raisins
15 ml (1 tbsp) toasted pine nuts

Below: Pan-fried Duck Breast on a Salad of Braised Red Cabbage

• Cook's Note •

Prepare the braised red cabbage a day ahead.

To prepare the braised red cabbage, heat the oil in a large pan and sauté the onion until soft, but not coloured. Add the red cabbage and cook, stirring, for 10 minutes.

Peel, core and chop the apple and add to the cabbage with the sugar. Cook for a further 5 minutes. Add the remaining ingredients and bring to a gentle simmer. Cover the pan and simmer very gently for 2 hours, adding a little more wine vinegar if the mixture becomes dry. Leave overnight at room temperature.

Sprinkle the salt into a heavy frying pan and heat. When hot, add the duck breasts, skin side down and sauté for 10 minutes; they will yield a lot of fat. Turn the breasts over and cook the meat side for 4 minutes until tender, but still pink inside. Remove from the pan. Leave in a warm place to rest for 10 minutes.

Meanwhile prepare the orange salad dressing. Finely pare the rind from half of the orange, cut into fine strips and reserve for the garnish. Squeeze the juice from the orange and mix with the vinegar, mustard and seasoning. Whisk in the olive oil to yield a thick emulsion.

Arrange the salad leaves on one half of each serving plate. Place 2 or 3 heaped spoonfuls of the cooled braised cabbage on top of the salad.

Slice the duck breasts into thin diagonal slices and arrange in a fan shape on the other side of each plate. Spoon the orange dressing over the duck and salad. Top with the raisins, pine nuts and the reserved orange rind to serve.

Mark James

Roquefort Tartlets

with a Walnut Salad

Pastry:

120 g (4 oz) flour
pinch of salt
60 g (2½ oz) margarine, in pieces
25 ml (5 tsp) boiling water

Filling:

150 g (5 oz) Roquefort cheese
150 ml (¼ pint) double cream
1 large egg, lightly beaten
30 g (1 oz) walnuts, ground
freshly ground black pepper

Salad:

assorted salad leaves
15 ml (1 tbsp) wine vinegar
30 ml (2 tbsp) walnut oil
25 g (1 oz) walnuts

To make the pastry, put the flour, salt, margarine and boiling water into a bowl and mix together using a round-bladed knife. (Using boiling water will allow you to use the pastry immediately.) Roll out thinly and use to line 4 individual flan tins. Prick the bases with a fork.

Crumble the Roquefort into a bowl, add the cream and mix until smooth. Add the lightly beaten egg and the crushed walnuts. Add pepper. Pour the filling into the pastry cases and cook in a preheated oven at 190°C (375°F) mark 5 for about 45 minutes.

Meanwhile prepare the salad leaves. For the dressing, mix the vinegar with salt and pepper, then add the walnut oil and whisk to combine. Toss the salad leaves in the dressing.

Serve the tartlets just warm, with the salad leaves. Garnish with the walnuts.

Anne May

"Wonderful also as a main course for lunch."

Loyd

Goat's Cheese Filos

with Salad and Red Pepper Dressing

Parcels:
175 g (6 oz) goat's cheese, de-rinded and diced
6 sun-dried tomatoes in olive oil, finely chopped
few thyme sprigs (leaves only), finely chopped
freshly ground black pepper
24 squares filo pastry, each 10 cm (4 inches)
75 g (3 oz) butter, melted
12 long chives

Salad:
2 handfuls salad leaves (including lettuce, rocket and watercress)

Dressing:
1 clove garlic, lightly crushed
2 thyme sprigs (leaves only), finely chopped
75 ml (5 tbsp) extra-virgin olive oil
15 ml (1 tbsp) red wine vinegar
15 ml (1 tbsp) chopped basil
sugar, to taste
1 red pepper

• COOK'S NOTE •

Keep the filo pastry moist by covering it with a damp tea towel. Without the dressing, and made a bit smaller, these filos would make excellent canapés.

For the filo parcels, mix together the cheese, sun-dried tomatoes and thyme; season with pepper. Brush 12 filo squares with melted butter, lay the other 12 squares on top and brush these with butter too. Divide the cheese mixture between the 12 double squares and bring the corners of the pastry sheets up over the filling to form parcels, pinching to close. Tie each one with a chive, brush with melted butter and place on a greased baking tray. Bake in a preheated oven at 190°C (375°F) mark 5 for 10-15 minutes.

To make the dressing, steep the garlic and thyme in the oil for at least 1 hour, then remove the garlic. Put the flavoured oil, vinegar, basil, salt, pepper and sugar in a screw-topped jar and shake vigorously to combine. Cut the red pepper in half lengthwise, remove the core and seeds and place, skin side up, under a very hot grill until the skin is blackened. Cover and leave until cool enough to handle, then peel off the skin. Finely dice the pepper and add to the dressing.

To serve, toss the salad leaves in the dressing and divide between individual serving plates. Arrange 3 filo parcels on each plate next to the salad.

Brian Glover

Left: *Goat's Cheese Filos with Salad and Red Pepper Dressing*

FRESH PASTA WITH CHICKEN LIVERS

AND LEMON SAUCE

Pasta Dough:

225 g (8 oz) strong white flour (preferably Italian wheat flour type oo)
3.75 ml (¾ tsp) salt
1 egg
1 egg yolk (egg white reserved)
small handful of flat-leaved parsley
small handful of chervil
5 ml (1 tsp) white wine
5 ml (1 tsp) olive oil

Sauce:

225 g (8 oz) chicken livers, trimmed
15 ml (1 tbsp) olive oil
250-300 ml (8-10 fl oz) homemade chicken stock
2-3 cloves garlic, crushed
25 g (1 oz) Parmesan cheese, freshly grated
45-60 ml (3-4 tbsp) double cream
strip of finely pared lemon zest, blanched
salt and freshly ground pepper

To Garnish:

flat-leaved parsley and chervil sprigs

COOK'S NOTE

Fresh pasta is at its best cooked and served immediately after making. It can, however, be left to dry for up to 30 minutes before cooking.

To make the pasta dough, put the flour, salt, egg and egg yolk into a food processor and work until evenly mixed. Add the herbs, wine and oil, then process briefly until the dough begins to hold together, adding reserved egg white as necessary to bind. Wrap in cling film and leave to rest in the refrigerator for 30 minutes.

Put the pasta dough through a pasta machine until thin and silky, then cut into tagliatelle. If you do not have a pasta machine, roll out the dough as thinly as possible and cut into long thin strips.

To make the sauce, cut the chicken livers in half. Heat the oil in a large frying pan, add the livers and fry, turning, for 2 minutes. Drain on kitchen paper, then place in a dish and leave to rest in a low oven, set at 150°F (300°F) mark 2, while preparing the sauce.

Pour the stock into the pan and simmer until reduced by about half. Add the garlic, Parmesan, cream and lemon zest; reduce, then add seasoning to taste. Pass through a sieve.

Meanwhile, cook the pasta in boiling salted water until al dente; this will take only 30 seconds if cooked immediately; up to 2 minutes if the pasta has been left to dry for a short while. Drain thoroughly.

Arrange the pasta in a twirl on each serving plate. Surround with chicken livers and pour the sauce over them. Serve immediately, garnished with torn parsley and chervil leaves.

Sue Lawrence

Grilled Polenta with Tapenade

and Goat's Cheese

Polenta:
10 ml-15 ml (2-3 tsp) salt
275 g (10 oz) polenta meal

Tapenade:
125 g (4 oz) black olives, stoned
1 clove garlic, crushed
20 ml (4 tsp) capers
50 g (2 oz) good-quality tinned tuna fish in oil, drained and flaked
6 canned anchovy fillets
30 ml (2 tbsp) chopped basil

Dressing:
45 ml (3 tbsp) olive oil
10 ml (2 tsp) red wine vinegar
2.5 ml (½ tsp) French mustard
15 ml (1 tbsp) chopped basil
1 clove garlic, halved
salt and freshly ground black pepper

To Serve:
125 g (4 oz) rocket and lettuce leaves, mixed
125 g (4 oz) goat's cheese, derinded
a little olive oil

To make the polenta, bring 1.75 litres (3 pints) water to the boil in a large saucepan with the salt added. When boiling, adjust the heat to a simmer and, stirring all the time, gradually add the polenta meal in a constant stream, avoiding lumps. When all the polenta is in, cook gently, stirring almost constantly for 45 minutes. Taste and add more salt if necessary. Oil a 2.5 cm (1 inch) deep baking tray measuring 23 x 30 cm (9 x 12 inches). Pour in the polenta, smooth out and leave for 3-4 hours to cool and set.

For the tapenade, simply whiz all the ingredients in a food processor or blender until they form a paste. Alternatively, pound the olives, garlic and capers in a mortar with a pestle to a paste, then work in the tuna, anchovies, and lastly the basil.

For the dressing, shake the ingredients together in a screw-topped jar and allow to stand for 1 hour. Remove the garlic, then shake well to combine dressing, just before serving.

To assemble the dish, turn out the polenta and cut four 5 cm (2 inch) circles or squares. Cut each of these in half horizontally. Place on a foil-lined grill rack and toast under a hot grill for 5-10 minutes until the edges begin to brown, turning once.

Thinly slice the goat's cheese. Spread the toasted polenta with tapenade, top with goat's cheese slices, drizzle over some olive oil and grill for 3 minutes. Toss the salad leaves with the dressing. Arrange on individual plates, with the polenta. Serve immediately.

Brian Glover

"Wonderfully simple – upmarket peasant food."

Sir Roy Strong

• Ingredients •

Polenta is quite tricky, and you must make sure that it's lump-free. It helps to sift the polenta into the boiling water using your hand. Once made, it is an ideal base for strong flavoured toppings.

Tagliatelle with Globe Artichoke

and Wild Mushrooms

Pasta Dough:

100 g ($3\frac{1}{2}$ oz) strong plain flour
pinch of salt
1 egg, size 3

Sauce:

1 large globe artichoke
lemon juice, for brushing
25 g (1 oz) butter
60 ml (4 tbsp) extra-virgin olive oil
1 clove garlic, crushed
few drops of white truffle oil
salt and freshly ground black pepper
4 pied de mouton and
4 trompette de la mort, cleaned
(or other wild mushrooms)

To Serve:

freshly grated Parmesan cheese

To make the pasta, put the flour into a blender or food processor with the salt. Add the egg and process briefly until the dough holds together and forms a ball. Turn onto a lightly floured surface and knead until the dough is no longer sticky, about 8 minutes. Put the dough into a polythene bag and leave to rest in the refrigerator for1 hour.

Divide the dough into 4 portions and flatten each one with your hand. Put it through the pasta machine, adjusted to the widest setting, dusting lightly with flour to prevent it sticking. Pass the dough repeatedly through the rollers, folding the sheet between each rolling and gradually narrowing the gap between the rollers so the dough is pressed firmly each time. When the rollers are set on the last but one notch on the handle, the dough should be silky smooth. Feed the pasta through the wider set of cutters to make tagliatelle.

Hang the tagliatelle up to dry for about 1 hour: either use a pasta dryer or hang the strips over a clean broom handle suspended between two chairs.

To prepare the artichoke, pull off the outside leaves and discard. Cut off the top 2.5 cm (1 inch), to remove the sharp tips. Slice the artichoke in half vertically and remove the choke. Rub the cut surfaces with lemon juice to prevent discolouration. Peel 2.5 cm (1 inch) of the stalk. Slice down through the artichoke very finely, so each slice includes parts of the stalk, heart and leaves.

To make the sauce, heat the butter and oil in a pan, add the artichoke slices and sweat gently over a low heat for a few minutes. Add the garlic and cook for a further 1-2 minutes. Add a few drops of truffle oil. Season with salt and pepper. Cut the wild mushrooms into long pieces, add to the pan and cook slowly for a further 1 minute.

To cook the pasta, have ready a large pan of boiling salted water. Add a few drops of oil, then add the tagliatelle and cook briefly for 1-2 minutes until al dente (tender but firm to the bite). Drain thoroughly.

Divide the tagliatelle between warmed serving plates and spoon over the artichoke and mushroom sauce. Serve immediately, with freshly grated Parmesan cheese.

Derek Johns

Below: *Tagliatelle with Globe Artichoke and Wild Mushrooms*

FISH

Red Mullet and Grilled Vegetables

with a Peppered Fish Sauce and Rouille

3-4 red mullet, each about 225 g (8 oz), filleted (bones and trimmings reserved for the stock)
salt and freshly ground black pepper
22 ml (1½ tbsp) olive oil

Stock:
fish bones and trimmings from the red mullet
1 onion, quartered
few parsley and thyme sprigs
300 ml (½ pint) dry white wine

Sauce:
30 ml (2 tbsp) olive oil
1 shallot, or ½ small onion, chopped
1 carrot, diced
2 cloves garlic, peeled
30 ml (2 tbsp) chopped flat-leaved parsley
1 bay leaf
30 ml (2 tbsp) tomato purée
large pinch of cayenne pepper, or to taste
600 ml (1 pint) dry white wine

> **• Cook's Note •**
>
> During the summer when samphire is in season, use it in preference to spinach, making sure it is well cleaned.

Rouille:
1 red pepper
2 cloves garlic, blanched
5 ml (1 tsp) tomato purée
15 ml (1 tbsp) olive oil
15 ml (1 tbsp) fresh white breadcrumbs
15 ml (1 tbsp) crème fraîche
large pinch of cayenne pepper, or to taste

Vegetables:
2 red peppers
1 aubergine
salt
2 red onions
1 fennel bulb
2 large courgettes
60 ml (4 tbsp) olive oil, flavoured with garlic and herbs to taste

To Serve:
225 g (8 oz) spinach or samphire
black olives, to garnish

Put all the ingredients for the stock in a large pan, bring to the boil, lower the heat and simmer for 15 minutes, skimming frequently. Strain through a fine sieve, then return the stock to the pan and boil to reduce to 150 ml (¼ pint).

To make the sauce, heat the oil in a pan, add the shallot, carrot and garlic cloves and sauté for 2 minutes. Add all of the remaining sauce ingredients. Bring to the boil, lower the heat and simmer for 15 minutes, then increase the heat and boil to reduce to 150 ml (¼ pint). Strain through a fine sieve and add the fish stock; set aside.

Season the red mullet fillets with salt and pepper and rub with a little olive oil. If they are large, cut the fillets in half.

Place all 3 red peppers, including the one for the rouille, on a baking sheet, drizzle with a little oil and bake in a preheated oven at 200°C (400°F) mark 6 for 25 minutes. Remove from the oven, place in a dish, cover and leave until cool enough to handle, then peel off the skins. Halve the peppers and discard the cores and seeds.

To make the rouille, put 1 red pepper in a food processor or blender with the blanched garlic and tomato purée and work to a purée. With the motor running, add the oil in a thin steady stream through the feeder tube to form a thick, glossy mixture. Turn into a bowl and fold in the breadcrumbs to thicken the rouille. Add the crème fraîche and season with cayenne pepper and salt to taste.

To prepare the vegetables, slice the aubergine into thick rounds, sprinkle liberally with salt and leave to degorge for at least 20 minutes. Thickly slice the red onions, to give 4 solid rounds from each one. Trim the fennel and cut lengthways into 8 slices. Cut the courgettes into thick slices on the diagonal. Slice the 2 red peppers into strips.

(Continued overleaf)

Right: *Red Mullet and Grilled Vegetables with a Peppered Fish Sauce and Rouille*

To cook the vegetables, place the onion and fennel slices on a baking sheet, drizzle with 30 ml (2 tbsp) of the flavoured oil and roast in the oven at 180°C (350°F) mark 4 for 20 minutes, turning once. Add the pepper strips for the last 5 minutes.

Rinse the aubergine slices thoroughly in cold water to remove the salt and bitter juices and pat dry with kitchen paper.

Heat a ribbed chargrill pan until smoking hot. Brush the courgette and aubergine slices with a little of the flavoured oil and chargrill in batches until just cooked; keep warm while cooking the remainder. (Alternatively, these can be roasted in the oven with the onions and fennel).

Blanch the spinach in boiling water until just wilted and drain thoroughly, pressing the spinach to squeeze out excess moisture; keep warm. Reheat the fish sauce and keep warm.

To cook the fish, heat 15 ml (1 tbsp) olive oil in a large non-stick frying pan and gently fry the fish fillets, flesh-side down, for 5 minutes, then turn and fry the skin side for 2 minutes.

To serve, place a small mound of spinach in the centre of each warmed serving plate. Arrange a selection of vegetables with the red mullet in a circle on top. Pour the sauce around the fish and vegetables. Add a spoonful of rouille to each portion and garnish with black olives.

Alastair Hendy

Scallops and Prawns in a Ginger and Citrus Butter Sauce

SERVED WITH STEAMED BABY VEGETABLES

16 large scallops, shelled
20 large raw prawns, shelled and deveined
lemon juice, to taste

Sauce:
5 cm (2 inch) piece fresh root ginger, peeled and sliced
170 ml (6 fl oz) Sauternes or other dessert wine
60 ml (4 tbsp) double cream
175 g (6 oz) unsalted butter, cubed
juice of ½ lemon
juice of ½ lime
salt and freshly ground black pepper

To Serve:
steamed baby vegetables, eg carrots, sweetcorn, courgettes, fine beans, cherry tomatoes

To Garnish:
dill sprigs
wild celery leaves
lemon and lime zest

First make the sauce. Put the sliced ginger and wine in a saucepan over gentle heat and allow to reduce very slowly, for about 30 minutes to about 15 ml (1 tbsp) syrup. Add the double cream and bring to the boil. Take off the heat and whisk in the butter cubes, two at a time. Strain, then add the citrus juices and seasoning to taste.

Cut each scallop in half and season with salt, pepper and lemon juice. Season the prawns with salt and pepper. Put the prawns into a steamer and gently steam for 2 minutes. Add the scallops and steam for 1 minute.

Remove the scallops and prawns from the steamer and arrange on heated serving plates. Pour over the sauce. Arrange the steamed baby vegetables on the plates, alternating colours for maximum effect.

Garnish with dill sprigs and dot with a few wild celery leaves. Sprinkle over a little lemon and lime zest.

Alan Spedding

"Like a bouquet of flowers. Very very nice, perfect scallops."

Michel Roux

Bouillabaisse with Rouille

selection of fish and shellfish for 4 generous helpings (see below)

Fish Stock:
125 ml (4 fl oz) olive oil
125 g (4 oz) onions, chopped
75 g (3 oz) leeks, chopped
4 cloves garlic, crushed
230 g (8 oz) can chopped tomatoes
1 bottle white wine
1.25 litres (2¼ pints) water
2 bay leaves
few parsley sprigs
2.5 ml (½ tsp) dried thyme
wedge of fennel bulb
2 large pinches saffron strands, soaked in water
long strip of pared orange zest
salt and freshly ground pepper
1.5-1.75 kg (3½-4 lb) fish bones, trimmings, shellfish carcasses and cheap fish

Rouille:
3 fat cloves garlic
½-1 red chilli pepper
1-2 slices white bread
45 ml (3 tbsp) extra-virgin olive oil

To Serve:
1 French stick, sliced and toasted
chopped parsley, to garnish

First, prepare the fish stock. Heat the olive oil in a large heavy stockpot or flameproof casserole. Add the onions and leeks and cook gently for 5 minutes until softened; do not allow to brown. Add the garlic and tomatoes, increase the heat slightly and cook for 5 minutes. Add the wine, water, herbs, fennel, saffron with liquid, orange zest and seasoning. Bring to the boil, add the fish bones and trimmings, and simmer for 30 minutes. Strain through a sieve, pressing the fish and vegetables to extract as much juice as possible. Reserve this stock.

> "Ought to blow the tusks off an elephant."
>
> Loyd

To prepare the rouille, crush the garlic using a pestle and mortar. Discard the seeds from the chilli, then chop finely. Add to the garlic and pound to a paste. Moisten the bread with a little fish stock, then work into the rouille. Pound in the olive oil, then add enough fish stock to give a smooth, thick paste.

To cook the bouillabisse, bring the fish stock to the boil. Add the fish in order of thickness. Cook, uncovered, transferring the pieces of fish to a serving platter as soon as they are cooked.

Serve the broth in bowls, floating a piece of toasted French bread spread with rouille on top of each one. Sprinkle with chopped parsley and serve with the platter of fish.

Nicole Sochor

• Ingredients •

It is said that it is impossible to make a real bouillabaisse outside the Mediterranean because you can't get the proper fish, but you can achieve a pretty good result.

Try to use at least six different varieties and ensure you have a fair amount of authentic fish – such as red or grey mullet, gunard and conger eel. Sea bream, bass, lemon sole, hake and John Dory are all suitable. Include some rascasse if you can get it, plus a good selection of shellfish – crabs, lobster, mussels, etc.

Tuna with Peppercorns

in a Port Wine Sauce

1 fresh tuna steak, about 700 g (1½ lb) and 3 cm (1¼ inch) thick
15 ml (1 tbsp) black peppercorns
15 ml (1 tbsp) plain flour
salt
15 ml (1 tbsp) oil
50 g (2 oz) butter
30 ml (2 tbsp) brandy

Sauce:
150 ml (¼ pint) ruby port
475 ml (16 fl oz) good chicken stock
150 ml (¼ pint) double cream

First prepare the tuna. Using a sharp knife, remove the tough outer skin and the large central bone from the steak. Discard any long bones around the stomach cavity of the fish steak too. The steak will separate neatly into 4 quarters, each providing a portion.

Coarsely crush the peppercorns using a pestle and mortar. Mix with the flour and a little salt. Use to coat the tuna pieces thoroughly.

Heat the oil and butter in a heavy-based pan, which is large enough to hold the pieces of fish in a single layer. When sizzling, add the tuna and cook over a brisk heat, turning to brown both sides.

Heat the brandy in a small pan until the vapour rises, then set alight and pour it, flaming, over the tuna. Shake the pan and tilt it to ensure the flames reach all parts of the pan.

When the flames die down deglaze the pan with the port, stirring well to scrape up the sediment. Simmer over a low heat for 10-15 minutes until the fish is cooked through and flakes easily. Lift the tuna portions from the pan with a fish slice and transfer to a hot plate; keep warm.

Place the frying pan over a high heat, add the stock and boil vigorously to reduce the liquid to a thick, syrupy consistency. Stir in the cream and simmer for a few minutes to reduce; the sauce should be fairly thick but still pourable.

Place the tuna steaks on hot serving plates and pour around a little of the sauce. Serve immediately, with new potatoes and a tomato and basil salad.

Angela Geary

Cook's Note

I prefer to use a tuna steak, cut from a large fish. If unavailable, you can use two smaller steaks, each about 350 g (12 oz) in weight.

> *"The tuna was a real success, really unusual and marvellously gamey. Lovely sauce as well."*
>
> Robert Carrier

Salmon Fillets with a Sorrel Sauce

and a Hot Salmon Mousse

1 salmon, about 1.5 kg (3½ lb), filleted and skinned
a little olive oil

Mousse:
1 egg white, chilled
200 ml (7 fl oz) double cream, chilled
salt and cayenne pepper
juice of ½ lemon, or to taste
45 ml (3 tbsp) chopped dill

Sauce:
1 shallot, chopped
50 g (2 oz) butter, chilled
90 ml (3 fl oz) dry vermouth
300 ml (½ pint) fish stock
1 handful sorrel leaves, shredded
50 ml (2 fl oz) double cream
salt and freshly ground pepper

Weigh the salmon fillets and remove 225 g (8 oz) from the ends and sides for the mousse. Cut the remainder into equal-sized slices across the fillet, allowing 2-3 slices for each portion.

For the mousse, blend the 225 g (8 oz) salmon in a food processor or blender until smooth. Add the egg white and cream and blend briefly until evenly combined. Season with salt and cayenne, and flavour with lemon juice to taste. Chill for at least 30 minutes.

Line the bases of 4 ramekins with lightly buttered greaseproof paper. Divide half the chilled mixture between the ramekins, sprinkle on the chopped dill, then top with the remaining salmon mixture.

Cover each ramekin with foil and place in a shallow baking tray half-filled with water. Cook in a preheated oven at 190°C (375°F) mark 5 for 15 minutes. Keep warm and turn out just before serving.

"A wonderful sorrel sauce – it doesn't overwhelm."

Sir Roy Strong

Meanwhile, make the sauce. Sweat the shallot in 15 g (½ oz) butter until soft. Add the vermouth and reduce rapidly until a few teaspoonfuls remain. Now add the stock and reduce again, skimming from time to time, until you have just over 150 ml (¼ pint). Strain into a clean pan.

Meanwhile, melt another 15 g (½ oz) butter in a pan, add almost all of the shredded sorrel leaves and cook gently for a few minutes. Add to the sauce with the cream and reduce gently. Season to taste with salt and pepper. To finish, whisk in the remaining chilled butter, a piece at a time, and the rest of the shredded sorrel.

Just before serving, fry the salmon fillets in a little olive oil for 1-2 minutes each side, or grill for 2-3 minutes each side. Arrange on warmed serving plates, with a mousse. Spoon on some of the sorrel sauce to serve.

Brian Glover

Cook's Note

It's worth getting wild salmon for this – it has a superb texture as well as flavour. The sorrel sauce is a classic French accompaniment to fish and – if you prefer to leave out the mousse – you will still have an excellent dish!

Prince of Wales Salmon

Fillets of Salmon Stuffed with Leeks

700 g (1½ lb) middle-cut salmon
30 ml (2 tbsp) wholegrain mustard
450 g (1 lb) leeks
50 g (2 oz) butter
15 ml (1 tbsp) tarragon leaves
salt and freshly ground pepper
15 ml (1 tbsp) dry white wine

Stock:
450 g (1 lb) white fish or salmon bones and heads
1 onion
1 leek, white part only
4 button mushrooms
25 g (1 oz) butter
100 ml (4 fl oz) dry white wine
1 bouquet garni

"Salmon and mustard is terrific."

Loyd

First prepare the stock. Discard the gills, then chop up the fish heads and break up the fish bones; rinse well. Chop the vegetables. Heat the butter in a saucepan and sweat the vegetables until soft. Add the fish heads and bones and sweat for 3 minutes. Add the wine, bring to the boil and reduce by half. Cover the contents of the pan with cold water, add the bouquet garni and simmer, uncovered, for 30 minutes. Strain the stock into a bowl.

Meanwhile, remove the skin from the salmon and cut out the bone, leaving the fillets attached at one side. Open out like a book, tweeze out any small bones then spread with the mustard and chill while preparing the stuffing.

Thinly slice the leeks, place in a saucepan with the fish stock and cook until soft. Drain, reserving the stock. Purée the leeks in a blender or food processor with the butter and tarragon until smooth. Season to taste.

Spread half of the leek purée over the mustard-coated inside of the salmon and sandwich together. Lay the salmon on a sheet of foil, sprinkle with the wine and seal the foil. Bake in a preheated oven at 200°C (400°F) mark 6 for 25 minutes, then leave to rest in the foil for 5 minutes.

Mix the remaining leek purée with the fish stock to make a sauce and reheat gently. Add the cooking juices from the salmon. Cut the salmon vertically into 4 portions. Place one on each plate and pour on a little of the sauce. Serve the rest of the sauce separately.

Kate Whiteman

Grilled Salmon Steaks

with a Dill, Cucumber and Green Peppercorn Sauce

4 salmon steaks
30 ml (2 tbsp) olive oil
juice of ½ lemon
salt and freshly ground black pepper

Sauce:
10 ml (2 tsp) olive oil
2.5 ml (½ tsp) finely chopped garlic
125 ml (4 fl oz) dry white wine
125 ml (4 fl oz) fish stock
2.5 ml (½ tsp) plain flour
150 ml (¼ pint) double cream
5 ml (1 tsp) green peppercorns in brine, drained
¼ cucumber, peeled, seeded and chopped
75 ml (5 tbsp) chopped dill

To Serve:
rocket leaves

First make the sauce. Heat the oil in a saucepan and lightly fry the chopped garlic, then add the wine and fish stock and reduce by half. Mix the flour with the cream, then add to the sauce and reduce for a further 2 minutes. Add the peppercorns, cucumber, salt, pepper and dill. Set aside.

Brush the salmon steaks liberally with the olive oil and lemon juice. Season with salt and pepper. Grill under a moderately high heat for 8-10 minutes, turning once.

Arrange a bed of rocket leaves on each plate. Position a salmon steak on top and pour on the sauce. Serve with new potatoes tossed in butter, and broccoli with sesame seeds.

Nicholas Hocking

Right: *Grilled Salmon Steaks with a Dill, Cucumber and Peppercorn Sauce*

Ballotine of Two Fish

with Cream of Leek Sauce

Ballotine:

250 g (9 oz) middle cut fillet of salmon, skinned
9 medium spinach leaves
1 egg white
salt and freshly ground black pepper
75 g (3 oz) unsalted butter, softened
175 g (6 oz) lemon sole, skinned
225 ml (7½ fl oz) whipping cream
225 ml (7½ fl oz) double cream
3 drops of hickory smoke (optional)
3 cooked slices smoked back bacon, cut into strips (optional)

Leek Sauce:

400 g (14 oz) leeks
100 g (4 oz) butter
450 ml (¾ pint) double cream
1.25 ml (¼ tsp) salt
plenty of freshly ground black pepper

Cut two horizontal slices from the salmon fillet, each about 3 mm (⅛ inch) thick. Lay side by side on a large sheet of greaseproof paper, cover with greaseproof paper and flatten to approximately 10 x 15 cm (4 x 6 inches). Chill.

Meanwhile blanch the spinach leaves in boiling water for 20 seconds, refresh in cold water and drain.

Purée the remaining salmon in a food processor or blender with half the egg white and salt, adding 40 g (1½ oz) butter, while the machine is running. Transfer to a bowl. Purée the sole with the remaining egg white, salt and remaining butter in the same way. Chill the fish purées for 15 minutes.

Stir the creams together. Return the salmon purée to the food processor or blender and gradually work in half of the cream adding it through the feeder tube. Add half of the hickory smoke flavouring at this stage if using. Repeat with the sole mousse, remaining cream and flavouring, if using. Chill the fish mousses for about 15 minutes.

Season the salmon fillets and cover with a thin layer of sole mousse. Add a layer of spinach leaves, then cover with another thin layer of sole mousse. At this stage you can add the bacon strips, if required, in a line down the middle.

Roll the fillet up like a Swiss roll, taking care not to handle it too much, and wrap tightly in greaseproof paper. Chill in the refrigerator. On a separate sheet of greaseproof paper, spread half of the salmon mousse and make a groove down the centre to accommodate the rolled fillet. Cover with remaining salmon mousse and shape into a cylinder. Wrap the ballotine in a double thickness of muslin and secure tightly. Tie loosely with string at 3 places to ensure even cooking. (The string should not be too tight as the mousse expands on cooking.)

Poach in salted and barely simmering water covered with a heavy cloth to keep the roll immersed for 35-40 minutes. Test after 35 minutes, inserting a long needle into the centre; the mousse is cooked if the needle feels lukewarm.

Meanwhile prepare the sauce. Finely slice the leeks into 3 mm (⅛ inch) rounds. Melt the butter in a saucepan and sauté the leeks for 5 minutes. Add the cream, salt and plenty of pepper and reduce over a medium heat to the required thickness (and strength of flavour). If a smooth sauce is preferred, purée in a food processor or blender, then pass through a fine sieve.

Unwrap the ballotine and cut into slices. Serve with the leek sauce.

Caroline Mugford

Brill en Papillote

with Fennel and Truffle Oil

1 large brill, about 1.25 kg (2½ lb), skinned and filleted
2 small fennel bulbs
1 courgette
20 ml (4 tsp) olive oil
4 thyme sprigs
salt and freshly ground black pepper
40 g (1½ oz) butter
4 drops of truffle oil, or anchovy oil

Cook's Note

Ask your fishmonger to skin and fillet the brill. For the papillotes you will need 4 large circles of baking parchment.

Trim the 4 brill fillets as necessary and check that all bones have been removed.

Trim and slice the fennel and cut the courgette into julienne strips. Steam the vegetables for 5 minutes.

Heat the oil in a large pan and gently fry the brill fillets for about 1 minute on each side until browned but not cooked through.

To assemble the papillotes, cut 4 circles of baking parchment, each about 30 cm (12 inches) in diameter. Fold each circle in half, then open out flat. On one half of each circle form a base of fennel and courgette julienne. Lay a fillet of brill on top and add a sprig of thyme. Season with pepper and add a knob of butter and a drop of truffle oil.

Melt the remaining butter. Brush the other half of each circle with water to moisten. Brush the edges of the circles with melted butter to help them stick together. Fold the moistened half over the fish and fold the edges of the paper tightly to seal. Place on a baking sheet and bake in a preheated oven at 220°C (425°F) mark 7 for 7 minutes until the fish is cooked through.

Transfer the papillotes of fish to warmed serving plates. Serve at once, accompanied by Parsnip Timbales with Asparagus and Broad Beans (page 114).

Ross Burden

Below: *Brill en Papillote with Fennel and Truffle Oil*

Fish Pie Dauphinoise

with an Anchovy and Mustard Sauce

Bouquet Garni:
1 leek, white part only
1 tarragon sprig
1 parsley sprig
few chervil sprigs
2 bay leaves
1 blade of mace

Pie Filling:
2 medium salmon steaks
225 g (8 oz) cod, coley, whiting or undyed smoked haddock fillet
600 ml (1 pint) milk
salt and freshly ground black pepper
450 g (1 lb) waxy potatoes, eg Fir-apple, Charlotte or Belle de Fontenay
50 g (2 oz) butter
2 cloves garlic, crushed

Sauce:
1 bay leaf
4 peppercorns
1 slice carrot
1 slice onion
40 g (1½ oz) butter
40 g (1½ oz) flour
4 anchovy fillets, finely chopped
15 ml (1 tbsp) French tarragon mustard
juice of ½ lemon

To Garnish:
coriander sprigs

To assemble the bouquet garni, split the leek in half lengthwise. Place the tarragon, parsley, chervil, bay leaves and mace between the two split leek halves. Secure with string.

Place the fish in an ovenproof dish, pour over the milk and add the bouquet garni, salt and pepper. Cook in a preheated oven at 180°C (350°F) mark 4 for 30 minutes until just tender; do not overcook. Meanwhile, parboil the potatoes in boiling salted water for 2-3 minutes only, then drain thoroughly.

Remove the cooked fish from the ovenproof dish, reserving the liquid, then remove any skin and bones. Carefully flake the fish and place in a bowl, then toss gently to mix.

Slice the potatoes very thinly, using a mandoline or food processor, leaving the skins on. Grease 4 individual 300 ml (½ pint) oval earthenware pie dishes with butter, then line with baking parchment. Trim the edges, then brush the inside of the paper with oil.

Cover the base and sides of the dishes with a layer of potato slices. Two-thirds fill with the fish filling and cover the top with several layers of potato slices. Dot with the butter and crushed garlic and bake in the oven at 190°C (375°F) mark 5 for 40 minutes.

Meanwhile make the sauce. Strain the reserved milk into a saucepan and add the bay leaf, peppercorns, carrot and onion slices. Slowly bring to the boil and simmer over a low heat for a few minutes, then strain. Melt the butter in a saucepan, stir in the flour and cook, stirring, for 1 minute. Gradually add the milk, stirring continuously. Cook for 2-3 minutes, then add the anchovies, tarragon mustard and lemon juice.

Turn the cooked fish pies out on to individual serving plates and surround with the sauce. Garnish with coriander sprigs and serve with a crisp salad.

Tim Souster

Halibut Escalopes

with Courgettes

575 g (1¼ lb) halibut fillet, skinned
salt and freshly ground black pepper
300 g (10 oz) courgettes
250 ml (8 fl oz) fish stock
100 ml (3½ fl oz) dry white wine
1 egg yolk
225 ml (7½ fl oz) double cream
30 g (1 oz) butter
30 ml (1 tbsp) fresh white breadcrumbs
30 ml (1 tbsp) freshly grated Parmesan cheese

Cut the fish diagonally into 6 mm (¼ inch) thick slices and season with salt and pepper; set aside. Cut the courgettes lengthwise into 3 mm (⅛ inch) slices, using a cheese slicer, then blanch in boiling water for a few seconds; drain thoroughly.

Combine the fish stock and white wine in a saucepan and boil rapidly to reduce by half. Meanwhile mix the egg yolk with 30 ml (2 tbsp) of the cream; strain through a fine sieve and set aside. Add the remaining cream to the stock mixture and reduce again by half. Remove from the heat and carefully stir in the cream and egg mixture; don't let the sauce cook again or it will separate. Season with salt and pepper to taste.

Brush 4 large flat flameproof plates with butter and sprinkle them with salt and pepper. Fold the courgette slices in half and arrange on the plates. Lay the thin slices of fish on top and coat with the sauce. Sprinkle with the breadcrumbs and Parmesan. Season with a little pepper and place the plates under a hot grill for about 1 minute or until the topping is golden brown and the fish is cooked through. Serve immediately.

Rachel Southall

> *"A really terrific combination... and the fish didn't lose its meatiness."*
>
> Rose Grey

Cook's Note

Rachel based this dish on an original recipe from Anton Mosimann's "Fish Cuisine", first published in 1988. If possible, get your fishmonger to bone and skin the halibut for you, but remember to ask for the bones and skin for your fish stock.

Fillet of Baby Halibut

with Fennel, Shallots and Roasted Red Pepper

1 red pepper
75 g (3 oz) butter
1 fennel bulb, sliced
4 shallots, sliced
salt and freshly ground black pepper
4 skinned baby halibut fillets, each about 125-150 g (4-5 oz)
½ lime
2 spinach leaves

Roast the pepper under a preheated hot grill, turning frequently until it is black all over. Place it in a covered bowl until cool enough to handle, then peel, remove the core and seeds, and dice the flesh.

Heat 50 g (2 oz) butter in a pan, add the fennel and shallots, cover and soften, without browning, for 10 minutes. Add the pepper, then season with salt and pepper.

Butter 4 pieces of foil, each about 30 x 40 cm (12 x 16 inches). Divide the fennel mixture between them, then top each with a halibut fillet, a squeeze of lime juice, a sprinkling of salt and a knob of butter. Fold the foil to make loose parcels, sealing the edges well.

Place the parcels on a heated baking tray and cook in a preheated oven at 200°C (400°F) mark 6 for 6-8 minutes, depending on the thickness of the fish.

While the fish is cooking, shred the spinach, immerse briefly in boiling water and drain thoroughly.

Place a fillet of fish on each plate, surround with the fennel mixture and top with a few strands of spinach. Serve immediately, accompanied by new potatoes.

Jan Gilberthorpe

FILLET OF SEA BASS

WITH GOOSEBERRY AND NUTMEG SAUCE

4 fillets of sea bass, each about 175 g (6 oz), with skin
melted butter, for brushing
salt and freshly ground black pepper

Sauce:
225 g (8 oz) fresh gooseberries, topped and tailed
150 ml (¼ pint) medium dry white wine
40 g (1½ oz) butter
2.5 ml (½ tsp) freshly grated nutmeg
soft brown sugar, to taste

First make the sauce. Put the gooseberries in a heavy-based pan with 45 ml (3 tbsp) water. Cover and cook gently over a low heat for 10-15 minutes until tender. Allow to cool slightly, then press through a nylon sieve to remove the skins and pips.

Return the gooseberry purée to the clean pan and add the wine, butter and half of the grated nutmeg. Bring to the boil, stirring occasionally, then add the remaining nutmeg and brown sugar, to taste; keep warm.

Place the sea bass fillets on a grill rack and brush with a little melted butter. Cook under a hot grill for about 8-10 minutes, depending on the thickness of the fillets, turning once during cooking. Season with salt and pepper to taste.

Arrange on warmed serving plates and spoon on the gooseberry sauce. Serve with carrot tagliatelle, broccoli florets and new potatoes.

Kerry Church

> "The sea bass was very simple and went well with the gooseberry sauce."
>
> James Galway

COOK'S NOTE

Make sure that all scales have been removed from the sea bass fillets.

Left: *Fillet of Sea Bass with Gooseberry and Nutmeg Sauce*

MONKFISH

IN A WHITE WINE SAUCE

450 g (1 lb) monkfish fillet
5 ml (1 tsp) salt
15 ml (1 tbsp) cornflour
2 egg whites
300 ml (½ pint) corn oil

White Wine Sauce:
2 slices of fresh root ginger, crushed, juice reserved
60 ml (4 tbsp) dry white wine
60 ml (4 tbsp) chicken stock
2 cloves garlic, crushed
5 ml (1 tsp) sugar
15 ml (1 tbsp) cornflour

To Garnish:
shredded spring onion

Cut the monkfish into small cubes. Sprinkle with the salt, then dust with the cornflour to coat lightly. Lightly beat the egg whites in a bowl with 7.5 ml (1½ tsp) of the oil.

Heat the rest of the oil in a wok or deep frying pan over a moderate heat. When it is hot, fry the fish in batches. Dip the cubes of fish in the egg white mixture, one at a time, then fry in the oil for 2 minutes or until crisp and golden on the outside and cooked in the middle.

Drain the fish on kitchen paper and keep warm while cooking the remainder. Clean the wok.

To make the sauce, combine the ginger juice, wine, stock, garlic and sugar in the wok. Blend the cornflour with 45 ml (3 tbsp) water, add to the wok and bring to the boil, stirring. Cook, stirring, for 1½ minutes until thickened.

Add the fish to the wok and heat through for 45 seconds. Serve at once, garnished with spring onion.

Betsy Anderson

Turbans of Salmon and Sole

with a Watercress Sauce

Turbans:
8 small salmon fillets
8 small sole fillets
salt and freshly ground white pepper
25 g (1 oz) butter, melted

Mousseline:
225 g (8 oz) mixed white fish fillets (bream, whiting, haddock, etc)
1 egg white, size 2
250 ml (8 fl oz) double cream
25 g (1 oz) pistachio nuts, chopped

Fish Fumet:
450 g (1 lb) fish bones, heads and trimmings
1 onion, chopped
1 carrot, chopped
1 leek, chopped
1 bouquet garni
250 ml (8 fl oz) dry white wine

Watercress Sauce:
25 g (1 oz) butter
25 g (1 oz) plain flour
600 ml (1 pint) fish fumet
½ bunch watercress

To prepare the mousseline, purée the white fish in a food processor until smooth. Add the egg white and process briefly until evenly blended. Transfer to a pyrex bowl and cover the surface closely with cling film. Place in a large bowl containing ice and refrigerate for 1 hour. Uncover and gradually work in the cream. Fold in the pistachio nuts and season with salt. Cover and refrigerate until required.

To prepare the fish fumet, put the fish bones, heads and trimmings in a large saucepan with the vegetables. Add 600 ml (1 pint) water, the bouquet garni and white wine. Bring to the boil, cover and simmer

gently for 20 minutes. Strain through a fine sieve and check the seasoning. Measure 600 ml (1 pint) for the watercress sauce.

To prepare the turbans, brush 4 individual baba moulds or dariole moulds with melted butter. Season the salmon and sole fillets and use to line the moulds: alternate the fillets and allow them to overhang the edges of the moulds by about 2.5 cm (1 inch). Pack the mousseline into the moulds and fold the overhanging fillets over the mousseline to enclose.

Cover each mould with a circle of greaseproof paper (cut to fit). Place on a wire rack in an ovenproof dish and pour enough hot water into the dish to come halfway up the sides of the moulds. Cook in a preheated oven at 170°C (325°F) mark 3 for 35-40 minutes until the turbans are set and springy to the touch. Remove from the oven and leave to rest for 10 minutes.

Meanwhile, make the watercress sauce. Melt the butter in a pan, stir in the flour and cook for 1-2 minutes. Remove from the heat and gradually stir in the fish fumet. Bring to a simmer, stirring, and cook, stirring, for 2-3 minutes until thickened and smooth. Set aside a few watercress sprigs for garnish; finely chop the rest and stir into the sauce; keep warm.

Remove the greaseproof paper from the moulds. Invert, one at a time, onto a plate, drain off any liquid, then invert onto a warmed serving plate. Soak up any remaining liquid with kitchen paper. Brush the turbans with melted butter and garnish with sprigs of watercress. Serve with the watercress sauce and creamed potatoes.

Tony Davis

Left: *Turbans of Sole and Salmon with a Watercress Sauce*

Sea Bass with Red Pepper and Basil Sauce

and Tomato Concassé

4 fillets of sea bass (preferably English), each about 175 g (6 oz)
olive oil for brushing
salt and freshly ground pepper
small handful of basil leaves

Tomato Concassé:
225 g (8 oz) ripe tomatoes (Italian plum or beefsteak variety)
handful of basil leaves, torn

Red Pepper and Basil Sauce:
2 red peppers, halved, cored and seeded
15 ml (1 tbsp) extra-virgin olive oil
5 ml (1 tsp) chilli-flavoured olive oil (optional)
15 ml (1 tbsp) chopped shallots
1 clove garlic, crushed
2-3 good handfuls of basil leaves
400 ml (14 fl oz) fish stock

Check over the sea bass fillets, tweezing out any small bones and removing any scales. Brush with oil and season with salt and pepper. Slash the skin of each fillet in 2 or 3 places and insert basil leaves in the slits. Cover with oiled cling film and leave to marinate for 1 hour or longer.

To prepare the tomato concassé, skin the tomatoes, then halve and remove the seeds. Finely dice the tomato flesh and add basil and seasoning to taste.

To make the red pepper and basil sauce, roughly chop the peppers. Heat the oils in a pan, add the shallots and garlic and cook gently until softened. Add the red peppers and basil, then add the fish stock and simmer, uncovered, for about 20 minutes. Transfer to a blender or food processor and work to a purée. Pass through a sieve. Check seasoning; keep warm.

Unwrap the sea bass fillets and cook under a preheated high grill, turning occasionally, for 5-6 minutes, depending on thickness. Transfer to individual plates, surround with the red pepper and basil sauce and top with a spoonful of tomato concassé. Serve immediately.

Sue Lawrence

Sue Lawrence – Winner 1991

Life has taken some fairly dramatic turns for Sue over the last two years. From being a busy Mum and part-time French teacher she has gone on to write two cookery books, "Entertaining at Home in Scotland" and "Cooking for pleasure". As a result she was thrilled to be admitted to the Food Writers Guild of Great Britain and has a weekly column in the Edinburgh Evening News. Sue's love of travel has taken her world wide since winning the competition. She has recently returned from a trip to Venezuela and has accepted an invitation to demonstrate Scottish cookery to some of Hong Kong's top chefs.

MEAT

NOISETTES OF LAMB
WITH THYME AND RED WINE

2 lamb fillets, each about 225-300 g (8-10 oz)
hazelnut oil, for brushing
handful of thyme sprigs
25 g (1 oz) butter
30 ml (2 tbsp) olive oil
salt and freshly ground pepper
150 ml (¼ pint) good red wine
300 ml (½ pint) strong lamb stock

Rub the lamb fillets with hazelnut oil and thyme. Place in a shallow dish, cover and leave to marinate for 1-2 hours.

Heat half of the butter and the olive oil in a heavy-based frying pan. Lightly season the lamb and fry, turning frequently, for 5-6 minutes depending on thickness. Remove from the pan and leave to rest in a low oven while making the sauce.

Add the red wine to the pan with a few thyme sprigs, stirring to deglaze. Add the lamb stock and reduce until syrupy. Stir in the remaining butter and check the seasoning. Strain through a muslin-lined sieve.

To serve, cut the lamb into noisettes; they should be pink inside. Arrange on individual serving plates and spoon the sauce around the noisettes. Serve accompanied by pasta, and spinach flavoured with nutmeg.

Sue Lawrence

LAMB WITH PORT
AND REDCURRANT SAUCE

4 portions best end of lamb (about 3 chops per portion)
50 g (2 oz) clarified butter
salt
30 ml (2 tbsp) olive oil

Port and Redcurrant Sauce:
150 ml (¼ pint) port
125 g (4 oz) redcurrant jelly
juice of 1 orange
juice of ½ lemon
5 ml (1 tsp) mustard powder
5 ml (1 tsp) arrowroot

To Garnish:
redcurrant sprigs

Cut out the 'eye' of the chops, removing fat and sinew. Rub with clarified butter and season with salt. Heat the oil in a frying pan and fry the lamb, turning, for a few minutes on each side, until browned on the outside, but still pink in the middle.

To prepare the sauce, put the port and redcurrant jelly in a saucepan and heat gently until dissolved. Add the orange and lemon juices. Stir in the mustard. Blend the arrowroot with a little water and add to the sauce. Heat, stirring, until the sauce thickens.

Cover about a quarter of each serving plate with the sauce. Slice the lamb thinly and arrange the slices overlapping in a fan shape on the sauce. Garnish with sprigs of redcurrants and serve with mangetouts and carrots.

Malcolm Hawe

"That's exactly how it should be – a great taste of olives."

Eugene McCoy

Right: *Lamb with Port and Redcurrant Sauce*

DRY-SPICED LAMB

10 ml (2 tsp) light olive or grapeseed oil
2 eyes of loin of lamb, each 275-350 g (10-12 oz)
5 ml (1 tsp) ground cumin
5 ml (1 tsp) ground cinnamon
5 ml (1 tsp) ground coriander
seeds from 4 cardamom pods, crushed
12 juniper berries, warmed and crushed
pinch of allspice
pinch of black pepper
10 ml (2 tsp) clear honey
2 ml (scant 1 tsp) powdered mustard
1.25 ml (¼ tsp) Dijon mustard
5 ml (1 tsp) white poppy seeds
5 ml (1 tsp) sesame seeds
5 ml (1 tsp) pink peppercorns, lightly crushed (optional)

Massage the oil into the meat, then coat with the spices and berries and sprinkle with allspice and pepper. Wrap loosely in foil and refrigerate for 12-24 hours. Shortly before cooking, brush off the juniper berries and smear one side of each piece of meat with 5 ml (1 tsp) honey, half the powdered mustard and the Dijon mustard. Put the two pieces of meat together, honeyed sides facing each other, thick end to thin, and tie firmly but not too tightly at regular intervals. Coat with the remaining mustard, poppy and sesame seeds, using a little honey or oil to 'stick' the seeds if necessary.

When ready to cook the lamb, place on a rack in a suitable roasting dish and roast in a preheated oven at 230°C (450°F) mark 8 for 12-15 minutes. To test, press the meat to check for resilience or insert the tip of a thin-bladed knife and check pinkness. Wrap in a double thickness of foil and leave to rest in a warm place for 10-15 minutes.

Slice the meat carefully into medallions, discarding the string. Arrange on warmed serving plates and sprinkle with pink peppercorns if wished. Serve with new potatoes and a warm spinach salad.

Silvija Davidson

COOK'S NOTE

This recipe was developed for a rare-breed lamb, which has a strong, 'dusky' flavour. Try to get well-hung meat, and omit honey if using new-season or spring lamb. One whole eye of loin is sufficient for two servings.

LAMB EN CROÛTE

WITH A PORT AND ORANGE SAUCE

25 g (1 oz) unsalted butter
2 fillets of lamb, each about 400 g (14 oz)
salt and freshly ground black pepper
18 large spinach leaves
450 g (1 lb) ready-made puff pastry
beaten egg, to glaze

Port and Orange Sauce:
150 ml (¼ pint) veal stock
150 ml (¼ pint) dry red wine
juice of 2 oranges
juice of ½ lemon
30 ml (2 tbsp) redcurrant jelly
1 shallot, finely chopped
1 clove garlic
2.5 ml (½ tsp) chopped fresh root ginger
1 thyme sprig
1 bay leaf
60 ml (4 tbsp) ruby port
65 g (2½ oz) unsalted butter, chilled and diced
salt and freshly ground pepper

COOK'S NOTE

The cooking time for this dish is critical. The pastry needs to be crisp and golden brown, while the enclosed lamb fillet should be pink and tender.

Heat the butter in a frying pan, add the lamb fillets and cook over a high heat for 2 minutes, turning to seal on all sides. Remove from the pan, season with salt and pepper and allow to cool.

Blanch the spinach leaves in boiling water for 5-7 seconds only, refresh in cold water, then drain. Lay out the spinach leaves in two lines, the same length as the lamb fillets. Lay a lamb fillet on each line of spinach and wrap the spinach leaves around each piece of lamb to enclose.

Cut the pastry in half. Roll out each piece to a rectangle and place a spinach-wrapped fillet in the centre. Brush the edges of the pastry with beaten egg and wrap each fillet in pastry, pressing the edges to seal. Place seam-side down on a baking sheet and leave to rest at room temperature for about 30 minutes.

Meanwhile to make the sauce, put all the ingredients, except the port, butter and seasoning, in a pan. Bring to the boil and boil to reduce by three quarters, skimming occasionally. Strain through a fine sieve, then return to the pan and reheat. Add the port and simmer for a few minutes.

To cook the lamb, brush the pastry with beaten egg and bake in a preheated oven at 200°C (400°F) mark 6 for 15-20 minutes, until the pastry is crisp and golden brown.

To finish the sauce, whisk in the butter a piece at a time on and off the heat, making sure each piece is thoroughly incorporated before adding the next. Season with salt and pepper to taste.

To serve, cut the lamb into slices and arrange on warmed serving plates. Spoon on the sauce and serve at once, with vegetables of your choice.

Richard Kuch

Rack of Lamb

in a Wine and Shallot Sauce

2 racks of lamb, each with 6 chops
30 ml (2 tbsp) olive oil
2 rosemary sprigs
2 thyme sprigs
salt and freshly ground black pepper

Wine and Shallot Sauce:
8 shallots, roughly chopped
1 thyme sprig
1 bay leaf
50 ml (2 fl oz) port
50 ml (2 fl oz) matured sherry vinegar
400 ml (14 fl oz) red wine
400 ml (14 fl oz) lamb stock
15 g (½ oz) cold unsalted butter, diced

Leek Garnish:
1 leek
groundnut oil, for frying

To Serve:
Horseradish and Ginger Rösti
(page 115)

First prepare the wine and shallot sauce. Combine all the ingredients, except the stock and butter, in a bowl or non-reactive pan and leave to infuse as long as time allows, but preferably overnight. Transfer to a pan if necessary and bring to the boil. Simmer until reduced by two thirds. Add the stock and reduce again by half. Strain through a fine sieve and work in the butter a piece at a time. Keep warm.

Heat the oil in a large frying pan until very hot. Sear each rack of lamb for 1 minute on each side and 3 minutes on its back. Transfer to a hot roasting tin, placing the rack on the reserved lamb bones. Lay a sprig of thyme and rosemary on each rack and roast in a preheated oven at 220°C (425°F) mark 7 for 12 minutes. Season.

To prepare the garnish, halve the leek and cut into fine julienne strips. Heat the oil to 140°C (285°F) and fry the leeks until pale golden in colour. Drain well on absorbent kitchen paper.

Leave the meat to rest in a warm place for a few minutes before carving into individual cutlets. Serve the cutlets on the horseradish and ginger röstis. Spoon the wine and shallot sauce around, and top with the leek garnish. Serve with a selection of baby vegetables.

Gregory Lewis

Cook's Note

The racks of lamb should be 'Frenched' – well trimmed and lean. Reserve any spare bones to make a trivet to roast the lamb on, or ask your butcher for a few extra bones.

"A great combination"

Loyd

Walnut-coated Best End of Lamb

2 best ends of lamb, preferably Manx Lochtan
a little extra-virgin olive oil
beaten egg yolk, for brushing

Coating:
100-175 g (4-6 oz) walnut halves
50 g (2 oz) brown sugar
15 ml (1 tbsp) chopped parsley

Sauce:
600 ml (1 pint) gamey lamb stock (see right)
15 ml (1 tbsp) good malty real ale
salt and freshly ground black pepper
knob of butter, to thicken

To Garnish:
3-4 firm pickled walnuts
flat-leaved parsley

To prepare the lamb, scrape the ribs until they are completely clean to avoid any scraps of tissue burning.

Put all the ingredients for the coating in a food processor and process until the mixture resembles fine crumbs, then spread out on a large plate.

Heat a little olive oil in a frying pan and sear the lamb joints on all sides, then place on the trivet of extra bones (or on a metal trivet) in a roasting tin. Roast in a preheated oven at 220°C (425°F) mark 7 for 8-10 minutes, then remove and brush the meat (not the rib bones) with egg yolk. Holding the rib bones, dip the meat in the walnut mixture to coat evenly. Put back on the trivet and roast for a further 8-10 minutes (depending on the size of the joint and how pink you like your lamb).

While the lamb is cooking, reduce the lamb stock by boiling until it is thick enough to coat the back of a spoon. Just before serving, add the ale and season well with salt and pepper. Remove from the heat and whisk in the butter. Keep warm.

Cover the lamb with foil and leave to rest for 5 minutes, then carve into cutlets. Arrange these on hot serving plates, spoon the sauce over the meat and garnish with sliced pickled walnuts and flat-leaved parsley.

Gamey Lamb Stock: Prepare this in advance. You will need 1 kg (2 lb) 'gamey' lamb bones, or include a pheasant carcass if using a domestic breed of lamb. Place in a roasting tin with 1 onion, quartered; 1 carrot, quartered lengthways; 1 leek, roughly chopped; and 2 tomatoes, halved. Roast at 200°C (400°F) mark 6 for about 15 minutes until well browned.

Transfer the bones and vegetables to a large saucepan and add 5 pints (3 litres) water, salt and a bouquet garni. Bring to the boil and simmer gently for 3-4 hours, skimming from time to time. Strain through a fine sieve and allow to cool. Chill, then remove any fat from the surface. Return to a clean pan and reduce to about 600 ml (1 pint) by boiling to concentrate the flavour.

Brian Tompkins

"The display was wonderful to look at. The whole thing has a tremendous appearance to it."

Michael Elphick

• Ingredients •

Lochtan lamb is a wonderful 'gamey' lean meat from a four-horned breed reared on an organic farm on the Isle of Man. You could however use traditional English or Welsh Lamb. Ask your butcher for some extra lamb bones if possible to use as a trivet for roasting the lamb. Get your butcher to 'French trim' the lamb, removing all bones except the 'fingers' of the rib bones for decoration.

Right: *Walnut-coated Best End of Lamb*

Noisettes of Welsh Lamb

4 large noisettes of lamb, each about 150 g (5 oz)
25 g (1 oz) butter, melted
75 g (3 oz) fresh breadcrumbs
15 ml (1 tbsp) finely chopped rosemary
salt and freshly ground black pepper
a little beaten egg yolk

Trim the chops of excess fat if necessary. Combine the melted butter, breadcrumbs and rosemary in a bowl and season with salt and pepper to taste. Coat the lamb on both sides with a very thin layer of beaten egg and cover liberally with the crumb mixture.

Place the noisettes in an ovenproof dish and cook in a preheated oven at 220°C (425°F) mark 7 for 20-25 minutes, depending on the thickness of the noisettes, until tender. Serve immediately, with fresh herb-flavoured pasta.

Kerry Church

Above: *Southdown Lamb Fillet with Garlic Sauce*

SOUTHDOWN LAMB FILLET

WITH GARLIC SAUCE

600 g (1¼ lb) lamb fillet, from the loin
salt and freshly ground black pepper
14 g (½ oz) butter
4 good thyme sprigs, leaves rubbed off the stalks

Garlic Sauce:
20 large cloves garlic (unpeeled)
200 ml (7 fl oz) milk
20 g (¾ oz) butter
5 ml (1 tsp) sugar
500 ml (16 fl oz) good lamb or chicken stock
150 ml (¼ pint) crème fraîche

Season the lamb fillet with salt and pepper. Rub all over with the butter, then with the thyme leaves, pressing them into the meat. Leave to stand for 20 minutes or longer if possible. Place in a lightly buttered roasting tin and roast in a preheated oven at 200°C (400°F) mark 6 for 10 to 15 minutes.

Vanessa Binns – Winner 1992

Having given up her career as a Kindergarten teacher, Vanessa is kept busy with public speaking engagements as well as writing articles for local newspapers and magazines. She enjoys giving cookery demonstrations, her newly refurbished kitchen being the latest venue. Vanessa is also involved in new product development and has travelled to Canada to make a film about the country's food. This year she has completed a series of pilot programmes for Radio Four.

"I think that is wonderful. I like everything about that."

Loyd

To make the garlic sauce, put the garlic cloves in a saucepan and cover with the milk. Bring to the boil and cook for 1 minute; drain.

Heat the butter in a roasting tin, add the garlic, season with salt, pepper and sugar and cook over a medium heat for 2-3 minutes, stirring constantly. Transfer to the oven and bake for 15 minutes, turning the garlic frequently. Wrap 8 of the garlic cloves in foil and reserve; peel the remainder and chop finely. Place the chopped garlic in a pan with the stock and crème fraîche. Bring to the boil. Simmer until reduce to the correct consistency; you should have approximately 400 ml (14 fl oz) liquid. Pass through a sieve into a clean saucepan, pushing as much of the garlic through as possible. Adjust the seasoning.

Place the reserved garlic cloves in the oven to warm. Carve the lamb into thin slices and season with salt and pepper. Spoon a little sauce on to each plate and arrange the lamb in overlapping slices on the sauce. Spoon a little more sauce over the lamb and position two garlic cloves on each plate to garnish.

Vanessa Binns

Moroccan Couscous

with Pumpkin

700 g (1½ lb) lamb (shoulder and knuckle)
4 large Spanish onions
225 g (8 oz) unsalted butter
1 chicken quarter
2.5 ml (½ tsp) turmeric
5 ml (1 tsp) ground ginger
2 pinches of pulverised saffron
10 ml (2 tsp) freshly ground pepper
salt
1.75 litres (3 pints) light lamb stock
450 g (1 lb) couscous
425 g (15 oz) can chick peas, drained
450 g (1 lb) carrots, cut into chunks
700 g (1½ lb) pumpkin, cut into chunks
175 g (6 oz) raisins
60 ml (4 tbsp) sugar
1 cinnamon stick

To Serve:
dash of rosewater
sprinkling of ground cinnamon
chopped coriander leaves
harissa sauce (available from delicatessens)

"This is better than the one I had in Morocco."

Anton Edelmann

Cut the lamb into 4 or 5 steaks. Halve the onions and slice lengthwise. Heat half of the butter in a large heavy-based saucepan or cooking pot. Add the lamb, chicken, onions, turmeric, ginger, saffron, pepper and salt and fry gently for 3-4 minutes, until lightly coloured. Add the stock, bring to the boil and simmer, covered, for 1 hour.

Meanwhile, empty the couscous on to a baking tray. Pour on about 600 ml (1 pint) water, then immediately strain off the water. Leave the moistened couscous to swell for 20 minutes, raking it with your fingers after about 10 minutes to separate the grains.

Place a tight-fitting steamer over the stew pan, making sure it stands well clear of the stew. Put the couscous into the steamer, and steam uncovered over the simmering stew for 20 minutes.

Return the couscous to the baking tray and sprinkle with a cup of cold salted water, containing 5 ml (1 tsp) salt. Let swell for 15 minutes, occasionally sifting with your hands to break up any lumps.

In the meantime, rub the chick peas to remove the skins, then add to the stew with the carrots, pumpkin, raisins and sugar. Return to a simmer and cook for at least a further 30 minutes. Replace the couscous in the steamer and steam over the stew for about 30 minutes. A few minutes before the end of the cooking time, add the cinnamon to the stew.

To serve, toss the couscous in the remaining 125 g (4 oz) butter and stir out any lumps. Sprinkle with rosewater and cinnamon. Spread the couscous on 4 warmed plated, making a well in the centre. Divide the meat into pieces and place in the centre of the plates. Ladle the stew over the meat and couscous and sprinkle with chopped coriander. Serve with harissa sauce.

Nicole Sochor

New Welsh Broth

2 loins or best ends neck of lamb, each 5-6 cutlets

Stock:
½ onion, chopped
½ leek, chopped
1 stick celery, chopped
25 g (1 oz) unsalted butter
salt
10 black peppercorns

Vegetables:
75 g (3 oz) leeks
75 g (3 oz) red onions
75 g (3 oz) Spanish onions
4 red cabbage leaves
8 Savoy cabbage leaves
50 g (2 oz) unsalted butter
salt and freshly ground black pepper
2 cloves garlic, halved
15 ml (1 tbsp) snipped chives
5 ml (1 tsp) shredded basil

Ask your butcher to remove the fat and take the meaty 'eyes' out of the lamb joints, or do it yourself. Keep the bones and meat trimmings.

To make the stock, sweat the chopped vegetables in the butter until softened. Add the lamb bones and trimmings and brown lightly. Add salt to taste, and the peppercorns. Cover with 1 litre (1¾ pints) water and simmer, uncovered, for 45 minutes. Strain and reduce by boiling to about 300 ml (½ pint).

Slice the leeks in half lengthwise and cut into 2.5-5 cm (1-2 inch) pieces. Quarter the onions. Then separate the leeks and onions into their natural layers, and cut the cabbage leaves into 5-7.5 cm (2-3 inch) pieces.

Melt 25 g (1 oz) butter in a heavy-based pan. Add the leeks and onions and cook until softened. Add the cabbage leaves and season with salt and pepper. Put the lamb on top of the vegetables, pour over the stock and bring to the boil. Cover the pan and simmer for 5 minutes only.

Transfer the meat to a warm dish, cover with foil and leave to rest in a cool oven at 110°C (225°F) mark ¼.

Add the garlic, 5 ml (1 tsp) chives and the basil to the vegetables. Cover and keep warm. Slice the lamb, adding any juices to the broth. Remove the garlic and stir in 25 g (1 oz) butter.

To serve, divide the vegetables and broth between 4 warmed serving plates and arrange the meat slices on top. Serve with new potatoes, tossed in butter. Sprinkle with the remaining chives to garnish.

Martin Benton

Cook's Note

I'm a great lamb fan, and I'm extremely happy to be within reach of the best lamb in the world! This is an adaptation of cawl, a traditional Welsh dish, although both Paul Bocuse and Anton Mosimann do similar versions. Poach the lamb for 5 minutes only – no longer – but allow to stand for at least 10 minutes afterwards, on a small plate, placed upside down on a larger one. This allows the juices to run down for you to collect, and stops the meat standing in its own juices.

Pork Fillet with Redcurrant and Port Sauce

2 pork fillets, trimmed
25 g (1 oz) butter
2 shallots, finely chopped
15-30 ml (1-2 tbsp) finely chopped sage
15 red pepper berries, crushed
pinch of ground mace
salt and freshly ground pepper
12 rashers streaky bacon, rinds removed

Sauce:
1 shallot, finely chopped
15 g (½ oz) butter
125 ml (4 fl oz) port
30 ml (2 tbsp) redcurrants
15 ml (1 tbsp) redcurrant jelly
squeeze of lemon juice (optional)

Cut a slice through each pork fillet, two thirds of the way along the length, so that you have two long pieces and two short pieces. Slit each piece horizontally, but do not cut right through the meat, so that you can open each piece of pork like a book.

Heat the butter in a pan and cook the shallots until softened. Remove from the heat and add the sage, pepper berries, mace and a little salt. Spread half the mixture on the opened surface of one long piece of pork. Position the two smaller pieces side by side on top. Cover with the rest of the shallot mixture and top with the remaining long piece of pork fillet, so that it looks like a large double-decker sandwich.

Stretch the bacon rashers with the back of a knife and line them up parallel and overlapping one another. Place the pork 'sandwich' on top of the bacon and wrap the bacon tightly round the pork. Place in a baking tin and cook in a preheated oven at 190°C (375°F) mark 5 for 1 hour.

For the sauce, cook the shallot in the butter until soft. Add the port and reduce slightly. Add the redcurrants, redcurrant jelly, salt and pepper. Adjust the flavour with lemon juice if required, then sieve.

To serve, cut the pork into slices and serve with the redcurrant and port sauce.

Gillian Stallard

Behind the Scenes...

"Our production team work overtime to see that everything goes well for MasterChef competitors. There are a few on and off screen disasters, but as in any kitchen fire is a persistent hazard. One competitor burnt her notes and another set a chopping board alight. Saucepan handles are regularly grilled in the heat of competition."

...Loyd

Spiced Pork Tenderloin

4 pork tenderloin fillets

Marinade:
60 ml (4 tbsp) chopped parsley
30 ml (2 tbsp) Mexican chilli powder
6 cloves garlic, crushed
15 ml (1 tbsp) cumin seeds
15 ml (1 tbsp) ground coriander
5 ml (1 tsp) ground cinnamon
200 ml (7 fl oz) red wine
30 ml (2 tbsp) red wine vinegar
generous pinch each of chopped oregano, basil and thyme

Sauce:
225 g (8 oz) butter
3 tomatoes, chopped
generous pinch of sugar
salt and freshly ground black pepper

Using the tip of a knife, make pinpricks in the pork fillets all over. Mix together the ingredients for the marinade in a shallow dish, then add the pork and turn to coat with the mixture. Leave to marinate for at least 1 hour, then drain, reserving the marinade for the sauce.

Place the pork fillets on a baking tray and cook on the top shelf of a preheated oven at 190°C (375°F) mark 5 for about 30 minutes.

To make the sauce, melt the butter in a saucepan, then add the reserved marinade, 500 ml (16 fl oz) water, tomatoes and sugar. Bring to a simmer and reduce until the sauce is slightly thickened and rich brown in colour; about 20 minutes. Adjust the seasoning.

Slice the pork fillets and arrange on warmed individual plates. Spoon over the sauce. Serve immediately with cardamom-flavoured rice.

Rose Gibson

Filet Mignon of Pork

with Leeks in Cider

750 g (1½ lb) pork tenderloin fillets
15 ml (1 tbsp) grapeseed oil
1 onion, chopped
½ bottle cider
4 small leeks, sliced
salt and freshly ground black pepper
20 ml (4 tsp) finely chopped lemon balm
250 ml (8 fl oz) double cream

To Garnish:
few lemon balm sprigs
snipped chives

Slice the pork diagonally across the grain into 8 thin or 4 thick slices. Beat the slices between sheets of greaseproof paper or cling film to flatten and tenderise the meat. Heat the oil in a heavy-based pan and quickly seal the meat on all sides. Transfer 2 thin slices or 1 thick slice to each of 4 large foil squares. Add the onion to the pan and cook gently to soften. Add the cider and boil for 2-3 minutes.

Spread the sliced leeks over the meat, pour over the onion and cider, season with salt and pepper and top with chopped lemon balm. Fold up the edges of the foil squares and fold together to enclose the meat. Bake in a preheated oven at 180°C (350°F) mark 4 for about 1 hour.

To serve, transfer the contents of the parcels to a warm dish and tip the juices into a pan. Cover the meat and leeks with foil and keep warm while preparing the sauce. Boil the juices to reduce and concentrate the flavour. Stir in the cream and heat through but do not boil. Taste and adjust the seasoning.

Pour the sauce over the meat and garnish with tiny sprigs of lemon balm and chopped chives to serve.

Rachel Rutter

Cook's Note

This is a family favourite. It's the sort of dish which won't come to any harm if your guests are a little late – just leave it in a barely warm oven and it will be fine. The sauce is easy to make but must be well reduced.

Stuffed Pork Tenderloin

with a Rosemary and Garlic Crust, served with a Madeira Sauce

900 g (2 lb) pork tenderloin (fillet)
12 fresh dates, stoned

Crust:
1 small bunch of rosemary
3 cloves garlic, chopped
50 g (2 oz) breadcrumbs
5 ml (1 tsp) salt
2.5 ml (½ tsp) freshly ground black pepper
50 g (2 oz) butter, melted

Sauce:
100 g (3½ oz) butter, diced
1 onion, chopped
50 ml (3½ tbsp) Madeira
350 ml (12 fl oz) chicken stock

To Garnish:
fresh dates
rosemary sprigs

"Cooking pork with rosemary is unusual but I thought it was very nice."

Hannah Gordon

Right: *Stuffed Pork Tenderloin with a Rosemary and Garlic Crust*

Trim any excess fat and sinew from the meat. Make an incision in the side of the fillet and fill with the dates.

To make the crust, strip the rosemary leaves from their stems and chop them finely; reserve half of the rosemary for the sauce. Place the other half of the rosemary leaves in the food processor with the garlic, breadcrumbs, salt, pepper and half of the melted butter. Process until evenly mixed, adding a little more melted butter if the mixture seems dry. Pat the mixture thickly over the pork and drizzle the remaining melted butter over the top. Roast in a preheated oven at 160°C (325°F) mark 3 for 45 minutes or until the juices run clear, when the thickest part of the meat is pierced with a fine skewer.

To make the sauce, heat 15 g (½ oz) of the butter in a saucepan and sauté the onion until softened, but not coloured. Add the Madeira, reserved rosemary and chicken stock. Reduce by half. Whisk in the butter cubes, one by one, making sure each piece is thoroughly incorporated before adding the next. Strain the sauce through a sieve and keep warm.

To serve, slice the pork and arrange on warmed serving plates. Garnish with fresh dates and rosemary. Serve with the Madeira sauce and vegetables in season.

Richard Kuch

PAN-FRIED TENDERLOIN OF TAMWORTH PORK

WITH A PRUNE AND ARMAGNAC SAUCE

• INGREDIENTS •

Tamworth is a particularly flavoursome breed of pig. If you are unable to obtain it, use any other well-flavoured pork.

2 pork tenderloins (preferably Tamworth), about 350 g (12 oz)
salt and freshly ground black pepper
16 prunes (preferably Agen prunes)
600 ml (1 pint) good homemade chicken stock
15 g (½ oz) clarified butter, for frying
120 ml (4 fl oz) Armagnac or brandy
150 ml (¼ pint) double cream

Season the pork tenderloins with salt and pepper. Put the prunes and stock in a pan and boil gently to reduce to just over 300 ml (½ pint). Remove the prunes with a slotted spoon and set aside half of them for the garnish. Remove the stones from the rest and pass through a sieve to form a purée, reserve the prune purée and stock.

Heat the clarified butter in a pan, add the pork tenderloins and sear over a high heat, turning to seal on all sides. Either transfer to a roasting tin and cook in a preheated oven at 225°C (425°F) mark 7 for about 10 minutes, depending on size, or continue to fry the pork in the pan, stirring frequently, until just cooked through but still moist.

Just before the tenderloins are fully cooked, pour on the Armagnac and set alight, shaking the pan to release the sediment on the base of the pan. When the flames die down, remove the pork from the pan, wrap in foil and leave to rest in a warm place for 5 minutes.

Add the reserved stock to the pan and boil vigorously until reduced to 150 ml (¼ pint). Stir in the prune purée to thicken the sauce and season with salt and pepper to taste.

Bring the cream to the boil in a separate pan and reduce by half. Add a tablespoonful of the purée sauce to impart colour. To serve, slice the pork and arrange on warmed serving plates on a pool of prune sauce. Pour on a little of the cream sauce and garnish with the reserved prunes. Serve immediately, with vegetable accompaniments.

Brian Tompkins

Left: *Pan-fried Tenderloin of Tamworth Pork with a Prune and Armagnac Sauce*

Oxtail in Port

with Root Vegetables and Hedgerow Jelly

1.5 kg (3 lb) oxtail
2 onions, sliced
150 ml (¼ pint) port
2 bay leaves
15 ml (1 tbsp) tomato purée
grated rind and juice of 1 orange
juice of 1 lime
1.2 litres (2 pints) oxtail stock (see right)
salt and freshly ground black pepper
225 g (8 oz) carrots, sliced
225 g (8 oz) parsnips, sliced
2 sticks celery, sliced
1 leek, sliced
15 ml (1 tbsp) hedgerow jelly

To Serve:
chopped parsley to garnish
Hedgerow Jelly (see right)

Trim the fat from the oxtail, then seal the meat in a hot heavy-based saucepan, without additional fat, on all sides. Remove and set aside. Fry the onions in the fat remaining in the pan until softened, then remove. Deglaze the pan with half of the port, stirring to scrape up the sediment.

Place the onions, oxtail, meat juices, bay leaves, tomato purée, fruit juices, stock and seasoning in a pressure cooker and cook for 45 minutes. Alternatively, cook in a flameproof casserole in a preheated oven at 190°C (375°F) mark 5 for 1½-2 hours.

If using a pressure cooker, transfer to a flameproof casserole. Mop up excess fat from the surface with absorbent kitchen paper. Add the carrots, parsnips, celery and leek with 15 ml (1 tbsp) hedgerow jelly. Add a little more stock if necessary. Cover and cook in a preheated oven at 180°C (350°F) mark 4 for about 45 minutes to 1 hour. Check the seasoning. Add the remaining port and reduce until the sauce has thickened slightly, on top of the cooker.

Serve sprinkled with parsley and accompanied by hedgerow jelly.

Oxtail Stock: Use the thinner tail ends, with fat removed, to make this. Place in a large pan with a few flavouring vegetables, ie onions, leeks, carrots, and a bouquet garni. Add water to cover, bring to the boil and skim the surface. Cover and simmer gently for 2-3 hours. Alternatively cook in a pressure cooker for just 30 minutes.

Hedgerow Jelly: Chop 1 kg (2 lb) crab apples, without peeling or removing the cores. Place the crab apples and 1 kg (2 lb) sloes (stalks removed) in a preserving pan with 1.2 litres (2 pints) water. Bring slowly to the boil, then simmer for about 1 hour. Ladle the fruit and juice into a scalded jelly bag over a bowl and leave to drip through for several hours.

Measure the juice and return to the preserving pan. Add 450 g (1 lb) sugar to each 600 ml (1 pint) juice. Stir over a low heat until the sugar has dissolved, then bring to the boil. Boil rapidly until setting point is reached; this will take approximately 10 minutes. Skim any froth from the surface, then immediately pot in hot sterilized jars.

Linda Yewdall

Calves Liver and Papaya

with a Madeira Sauce

4 thin slices calves liver, each about 75-125 g (3-4 oz)
15 ml (1 tbsp) flour
salt and freshly ground pepper
50 g (2 oz) clarified butter
25 g (1 oz) shallots, finely chopped
150 ml (¼ pint) medium dry Madeira
150 ml (¼ pint) veal stock
50 g (2 oz) unsalted butter, chilled and diced
1 papaya, thinly sliced

Coat the liver lightly with flour and seasoning. Heat the clarified butter in a frying pan. When it is very hot, add the calves liver and cook over a high heat for 1 minute on each side. Transfer to a plate and keep warm.

Sauté the shallots in the same pan until soft, then add the Madeira and boil until reduced by half. Add the stock and boil until the sauce is a little syrupy. Pass the sauce through a sieve into a clean pan and whisk in the chilled butter, a little at a time, over a low heat. Season to taste.

Place the calves liver on individual plates and pour over the sauce. Arrange the papaya slices around the liver and serve immediately, accompanied by a Mixed Leaf and Walnut Salad (page 104).

Amita Baldock

Tian of Beef Niçoise

4 large tomatoes
1 small onion
60 ml (4 tbsp) olive oil
salt and freshly ground black pepper
15 ml (1 tbsp) chopped basil
450 g (1 lb) fresh spinach leaves
freshly grated nutmeg
50 g (2 oz) butter
225 g (8 oz) button mushrooms
300 g (10 oz) beef fillet, in one piece
6 cloves garlic

Sauce:
170 ml (6 fl oz) red wine
300 ml (10 fl oz) beef stock
salt and freshly ground black pepper
50 g (2 oz) butter, diced

To Garnish:
parsley or other fresh herb sprigs

Skin, halve and seed the tomatoes, then chop coarsely. Chop the onion. Heat 30 ml (2 tbsp) of the oil in a saucepan. Add the onion and tomatoes and allow to sweat until the moisture has evaporated and the tomatoes are softened and mashable. Season with salt and pepper and flavour with the chopped basil.

Devein the spinach. Blanch briefly in boiling water, then drain and refresh. Squeeze out as much moisture as possible, then chop. Add a little grated nutmeg to taste and sauté in a little of the butter until just tender. Remove from the heat.

Chop the mushrooms finely and sauté in a little oil until they release their liquid. Remove from the heat.

Cut the fillet of beef down the centre line. Tie each piece of beef with string to hold its shape. Melt the remaining butter in a frying pan, add the garlic and sauté each piece of beef for 4-5 minutes, turning to brown evenly, until it is cooked but still pink inside. Wrap the beef in foil and keep warm. Reserve the garlic.

To make the sauce, deglaze the pan by adding the red wine and stirring to scrape up the sediment. Simmer to reduce to approximately 10 ml (2 tsp). Add the stock, salt and pepper, and bring to the boil. Reduce by one quarter, then strain into a clean pan; keep warm.

"*Love this combination... Very refined.*"

Loyd

To assemble the tian, reheat each of the vegetables. Rub a little of the fried garlic on the base of each plate and place a metal ring (ie a muffin ring or scone cutter) in the centre of each. Put the spinach in the bottom of the rings, in a fine layer, pressing down with a fork to spread and pack well. Cover with a layer of mushrooms, then place the tomatoes on top. Slice the beef finely and arrange on top of the tomato, to resemble the spokes of a wheel.

Quickly stir the 50 g (2 oz) diced butter into the hot sauce. Spoon a little on the top and around the base of each tian. Carefully remove the ring. Garnish with parsley or other herb sprigs.

Jane O'Sullivan

Behind the Scenes...

"It is – I think – very difficult to come up with a completely original dish. In the course of the series we've witnessed some supremely clever twists on old standbys: my favourite was a bread and butter pudding made with teacakes. My own feeling is that it's better for a cook to be good than to be original. But, I have been consistently impressed by the number of times that our chef judges have asked for details of our contestants' recipes. Who knows how many MasterChef recipes are now cropping up on top restaurant menus?" **...Loyd**

Right: *Tian of Beef Niçoise*

DAMBUSTER STEAK

450 g (1 lb) rump steak
50 g (2 oz) butter
30 ml (2 tbsp) olive oil
1 clove garlic, crushed
15 ml (1 tbsp) flour
30 ml (2 tbsp) brandy
¼-½ bottle red wine
150 ml (¼ pint) strong beef stock
salt and freshly ground black pepper
1 bouquet garni (parsley, thyme and 1 bay leaf)
125 g (4 oz) button mushrooms
½ small tin smoked mussels, drained

Yorkshire Puddings:
125 g (4 oz) plain white flour
pinch of salt
2 eggs
about 150 ml (¼ pint) milk (more may be needed)
15 ml (1 tbsp) oil

COOK'S TIP

I love to bring old English recipes up to date and this is based on a very traditional English dish of course. Remember, the secret of Yorkshire puddings is to have the fat as hot as possible in the trays.

Cut the beef into 2.5 cm (1 inch) cubes. Melt 40 g (1½ oz) butter with the oil in a large flameproof casserole or heavy-based pan. Brown the beef, add the crushed garlic, sprinkle on the flour and stir until thoroughly hot. Sprinkle on the brandy and ignite. Add 150 ml (¼ pint) wine and the stock and bring to the boil. Season lightly with salt and pepper, and add the bouquet garni. Cover and simmer very gently for 1½ hours, adding more wine if necessary. After this time the sauce should be sufficiently reduced.

To make the Yorkshire puddings, sift the flour and salt together into a bowl. Make a well in the centre, break in the eggs and add half the milk. Stir well, then add the remaining milk, whisking vigorously: the batter should be the consistency of double cream; add a little more milk if needed. Leave to stand for 1 hour.

Oil the Yorkshire pudding tins and place in a preheated oven at 220°C (425°F) mark 7 until very hot. Pour in the batter and cook for 15-20 minutes, until golden brown and well risen.

Meanwhile cook the mushrooms in the remaining 15 g (½ oz) butter in a frying pan for 2 minutes. Add to the steak, along with the smoked mussels, and cook for a further 10 minutes. Transfer the Yorkshire puddings to warmed serving plates and fill with steak, mushrooms and mussels. Serve with minted new potatoes and lightly cooked vegetable julienne.

Carol Alexander

MEDALLIONS OF BEEF IN MADEIRA

AND RED WINE SAUCE, WITH A MUSHROOM AND SHALLOT GARNISH

4 fillet steaks, each about 175 g (6 oz)
5 ml (1 tsp) unsalted butter
5 ml (1 tsp) sunflower oil
salt and freshly ground black pepper

Sauce:
8 shallots, finely chopped
1 thyme sprig
1 bay leaf
50 ml (3½ tbsp) Madeira
50 ml (3½ tbsp) red wine vinegar
400 ml (14 fl oz) full-bodied red wine
300 ml (½ pint) veal stock
100 ml (3½ fl oz) chicken stock
5 g (¼ oz) cold unsalted butter, diced

Shallot Garnish:
32 shallots (or 16 shallots and 16 baby onions), topped and tailed
30 g (1 oz) unsalted butter
1 thyme sprig
½ bay leaf
rock salt for baking
pinch of caster sugar

Mushroom Garnish:
50 g (2 oz) unsalted butter
10 ml (2 tsp) finely chopped shallot
225 g (8 oz) assorted mushrooms, cleaned and dried
2 tomatoes, peeled, seeded and diced
15 ml (1 tbsp) chopped chives

First make the sauce. Combine all the ingredients in a bowl, except the stock and butter. Add salt and pepper. Leave to infuse for several hours, or preferably overnight if time. Transfer to a saucepan, bring to the boil and reduce by two thirds. Add the stock and reduce by half. Remove the herbs. Add the butter and stir well until combined. Adjust the seasoning if necessary.

To prepare the shallot garnish, put 16 shallots in a foil parcel with 15 g (½ oz) butter, the thyme, bay leaf and a pinch of salt. Place on a bed of rock salt on a baking sheet and bake in a preheated oven at 220°C (425°F) mark 7 for 20-30 minutes until soft and shiny.

Peel the remaining 16 shallots or onions, melt the remaining 15 g (½ oz) butter in a sauté pan, then add the peeled shallots, sugar, salt and pepper. Cook until lightly browned, then cover with buttered greaseproof paper and cook in the oven for 20 minutes, stirring occasionally, until golden brown.

To prepare the mushroom garnish, melt half of the butter in a pan and sweat the shallot until soft but not coloured. Add the mushrooms and cook for 1 minute. If they release a lot of moisture drain in a colander, then return to the pan. Add the remaining butter and cook for a further 1 minute. Just before serving, add the chopped tomatoes and chives.

To cook the steaks, heat the butter and oil in a frying pan and sear the steaks over high heat for 2 minutes on each side, then cook for a further few seconds on each side. Season with salt and pepper. Place in the preheated oven for approximately 6 minutes, for medium rare steaks.

To serve, reheat the sauce. Slice each steak into 4 to 6 slices, depending on size. Arrange on warmed serving plates. Add the mushroom and shallot garnishes and pour the sauce around. Serve with Gâteaux of Vegetables (page 116).

Gregory Lewis

Fillet of Beef

with Juniper and Thyme Sauce

700 g (1½ lb) fillet of beef, in one piece
¼ bottle of Madeira
¼ bottle of red wine
small bunch of herbs, ie thyme, parsley, chives, finely chopped
salt and freshly ground black pepper

Sauce:
beef bones
1 carrot, finely chopped
1 onion, finely chopped
1 celery stalk, finely chopped
25 g (1 oz) thyme leaves, chopped
12 juniper berries, crushed

First prepare the sauce. Place the beef bones in a roasting tin and cook in a preheated oven at 190°C (375°F) mark 5 for 30 minutes to brown; reserve the cooking juices. Transfer the bones to a large stock pot or heavy-based pan and add the carrot, onion, celery, thyme and juniper berries. Add sufficient water to cover, bring to the boil and reduce to 300 ml (½ pint) liquid, then strain through a sieve.

Place the reserved meat juices from the roasting tin in a clean saucepan and cook over a moderate heat for 3-4 minutes. Add the stock a little at a time, because you may only require 150 ml (¼ pint), and season with salt and pepper. Reduce to a coating thickness and pass through a sieve again. Heat through before serving.

Place the beef fillet in a shallow roasting tin with the Madeira and red wine. Roast in the preheated oven at 190°C (375°F) mark 5 for 15 minutes per 500 g (1 lb) for rare, or 20-25 minutes per 500 g (1 lb) for medium, basting occasionally with the juices. Turn off the oven, open the door and leave to rest for approximately 30 minutes.

After resting, roll the beef fillet in finely chopped herbs. Carve into slices and serve with the juniper and thyme sauce, roasted parsnips and broccoli florets.

Caryl Doherty

Cook's Note

Make sure you use well-hung beef for this dish.

Gregory Lewis – Semi-finalist 1992

Gregory was only sixteen when he reached the semi-finals of MasterChef in 1992. He has since become an apprentice at the Connaught Hotel in Mayfair under the expert guidance of Maitre Chef de Cuisine Michel Bourdin. Gregory hopes to reach the top of his profession as a chef.

BOEUF EN CROUTE

WITH SMOKED OYSTERS

4 fillet steaks, each about 150 g (5 oz)
25 g (1 oz) butter
4 shallots, finely chopped
450 g (1 lb) packet puff pastry
105 g (3½ oz) can smoked oysters, drained and chopped
15-30 ml (1-2 tbsp) finely chopped parsley
1 egg yolk, beaten, to glaze

Sauce:
1.2 litres (2 pints) good quality beef stock (made from 2 marrow bones)
30-45 ml (2-3 tbsp) Madeira
50 g (2 oz) butter, chilled
salt and freshly ground pepper
lemon juice, to taste

Trim the fillet steaks. Heat the butter in a frying pan, add the steaks and seal very quickly on both sides, then remove. Add the shallots to the pan and sauté until lightly browned; remove.

Divide the pastry into 4 equal pieces. Roll out each piece on a lightly floured surface to a rectangle, about 25 x 12cm (10 x 5 inches). Place a steak on one side of each pastry rectangle and top with the chopped oysters, shallots and parsley. Brush the edges of the pastry with beaten egg yolk. Fold the pastry over the steak and press the edges together to seal. Use a 15cm (6 inch) fluted cutter to cut these edges into a scallop shape.

Brush all over with beaten egg yolk and decorate with leaves cut from the pastry trimmings. Place the parcels on a lightly buttered baking sheet and chill for 1 hour.

Meanwhile, heat the stock in a saucepan and simmer until reduced to about 150 ml (¼ pint) and thickened. Flavour with the Madeira.

Bake the parcels in a preheated oven at 220°C (425°F) mark 7 for 20 minutes until the pastry is crisp and golden.

Shortly before the steaks are cooked, add the butter, in pieces, to the stock, a little at a time, whisking constantly. Season with salt and pepper and add lemon juice to taste. Serve the steak parcels as soon as they are cooked, with the sauce, and vegetable accompaniments.

Robert Howlett

COOK'S TIP

Use well hung fillet steaks, and a good quality stock for the sauce. To ensure the fillet steaks are perfectly cooked, it is essential to chill the parcels before baking, and to serve them as soon as they are cooked. When cut open, the fillet steaks should be pink inside.

FILLET OF BEEF

WITH CHERRY AND BERRY SAUCE

700 g-1 kg (1½-2 lb) fillet of beef
about 30 ml (2 tbsp) hazelnut oil
salt and freshly ground black pepper
4-5 slices streaky bacon, derinded
125 g (4 oz) morello cherries
50 g (2 oz) sugar
squeeze of lemon juice
about 15 ml (1 tbsp) sloe gin (see below)
about 15 ml (1 tbsp) elderberry syrup (see right)
300 ml (½ pint) beef stock
25 g (1 oz) butter, in pieces

"An invention worth inventing"

Loyd

• INGREDIENTS •

To make your own sloe gin, prick 450 g (1 lb) sloes. Use to half-fill 2 clean dry wine bottles, then add the same weight of sugar. Top up with gin, cork and leave for at least 3 months. Decant to use.

***Right:** Fillet of Beef with Cherry and Berry Sauce*

Brush the beef with hazelnut oil, season with salt and pepper and wrap in the bacon slices. Leave to marinate for 1 hour. Heat 15 ml (1 tbsp) hazelnut oil in a frying pan and seal the beef on all sides over a high heat. Transfer to a roasting tin and cook in a preheated oven at 220°C (425°F) mark 7 for 20 minutes or according to taste.

Meanwhile put the cherries in a saucepan with the sugar, 30-45 ml (2-3 tbsp) water and a squeeze of lemon juice. Cover and cook gently until the cherries are tender. Strain off the juice, reserving the cherries.

Transfer the beef to a warmed dish. Deglaze the roasting tin with the cherry juice, then add the sloe gin and elderberry syrup to taste. Add the stock and reduce to a sauce consistency. Stir in the butter a little at a time, then strain into a clean pan. Add the cherries to the sauce.

Carve the fillet of beef into slices and arrange on warmed plates. Pour the sauce over the meat and serve with Parsley Profiteroles (page 106) and vegetable accompaniments.

Elderberry Syrup: De-stem, wash and drain the elderberries, then put in a pan with just enough water to cover. Simmer for 30 minutes. Strain through muslin into a clean pan. To each 600 ml (1 pint) add 450 g (1 lb) sugar and 10 cloves. Heat, stirring, until the sugar dissolves, then boil steadily for 10 minutes. Leave until cold, then pour into sterilized bottles.

Linda Yewdall

POULTRY & GAME

CHICKEN WITH ROAST GARLIC

IN SAUTERNES SAUCE

1 boned chicken, cut into 4 pieces (use carcass for sauce)
120 ml (4 fl oz) crème fraîche
4 baby carrots, scrubbed

Sauternes Sauce Base:
30 ml (2 tbsp) olive oil
450 g (1 lb) onions, sliced
450 g (1 lb) carrots, sliced
1 leek, sliced
1 chicken carcass, in pieces
1 kg (2 lb) veal bones
1 bottle Sauternes
450 ml (¾ pint) light chicken stock
bouquet garni, ie parsley sprigs, 2 thyme sprigs, celery and bay leaves
75 ml (5 tbsp) double cream
salt and freshly ground black pepper
10 ml (2 tbsp) lemon juice, or to taste

Roast Garlic:
2 heads garlic, unpeeled
15 g (½ oz) butter
10 ml (2 tsp) sugar

To Finish:
15 ml (1 tbsp) chopped parsley

•COOK'S NOTE•

This is an exceptional and extravagant main course! Most of the work is in the preparation of the Sauternes sauce base, which can be made in advance. The grilled chicken is tenderised by the crème fraîche, and the garlic is sweet and tender – not at all powerful or pungent.

Place the chicken in a dish, pour over the crème fraîche and season with salt and pepper to taste. Leave to marinate in a cool place while preparing the sauce.

To make the Sauternes sauce base, heat the oil in a large pan and add the onions, carrots and leek. Cover and cook for 5 minutes, then uncover and cook for about 15 minutes until browned. Add the chicken carcass and veal bones. Cook for about 10 minutes until browned.

Add a cupful of Sauternes and cook for about 20 minutes until reduced to a glaze. Repeat until all the Sauternes is used. Lower the heat and add the stock and bouquet garni. Cover and cook for 1 hour. Strain through a fine sieve, pressing to extract as much juice as possible. Cook until reduced to a cupful, about 10 minutes. Allow to cool, then remove any fat from the surface.

To prepare the garlic, add to a small pan of boiling water and boil for 3 minutes, then drain and remove the skins. Heat the butter in an ovenproof dish, add the garlic and sprinkle with the sugar. Cook in a preheated oven at 120°C (250°F) mark ½ (or at the bottom of a hotter oven while other dishes cook) for about 2 hours. The garlic should be tender and golden; if necessary cover with foil during cooking to prevent browning.

Cook the chicken under a preheated grill for 5-10 minutes, then turn over and grill for 5-10 minutes until tender and cooked through. Remove the chicken as it is cooked; the legs will take longer.

Meanwhile cook the carrots in salted water for 1 minute; drain.

Bring the sauce to the boil, then add the cream and reduce slightly. Correct the seasoning and add lemon juice if necessary. Slice the chicken attractively and arrange on individual serving plates.

Spoon over the sauce and garnish with the carrots, roast garlic and parsley. Serve with tagliatelle flavoured with tarragon.

Orlando Murrin

"I would be very happy just to have that and wish it were waiting for me at home."

Jean Marsh

Right: *Chicken with Roast Garlic in Sauternes Sauce*

Breast of Chicken

with Comté Cheese Sauce

4 boneless chicken breasts, skinned
salt and freshly ground black pepper
flour, for coating
60 g (2½ oz) butter
350 ml (12 fl oz) dry white wine
300 ml (½ pint) chicken stock
pinch of freshly grated nutmeg
pinch of cayenne pepper

Comté Cheese Sauce:
45 g (1¼ oz) butter
25 g (1 oz) plain flour
2 egg yolks
150 ml (¼ pint) crème fraîche
30 g (1 oz) Comté cheese, finely grated

To Finish:
60 g (2-2½ oz) Comté cheese, grated
blanched red pepper diamonds (see note)

Cut the chicken breasts into bite-sized pieces. Season with salt and pepper and coat evenly with flour, shaking off any excess. Heat the butter in a wide, shallow pan and brown the chicken pieces on all sides over a medium heat. Stir in the white wine; bring to the boil, then add the chicken stock with the nutmeg and cayenne. Bring to a simmer and gently poach the chicken pieces for a few minutes until tender. Remove the chicken with a slotted spoon and transfer to a greased 1.5 litre (2½ pint) baking dish. Skim off the fat from the cooking liquid. Strain the liquid and reserve.

To make the sauce, melt the butter in a saucepan and stir in the flour. Let it bubble for 1 minute, then gradually whisk in the strained cooking liquid. Simmer, stirring occasionally, for 5-10 minutes until thickened to a coating consistency. Check the seasoning.

In a bowl, beat the egg yolks with the crème fraîche. Whisk a little of the sauce into the yolk mixture, then whisk this mixture into the remaining sauce. Heat gently, without boiling, until slightly thickened. Remove from the heat and add the Comté cheese, stirring until melted. Check the seasoning.

Pour the sauce over the chicken. Sprinkle with grated cheese and bake in a preheated oven at 220°C (425°F) mark 7 for 5 minutes until golden brown.

Arrange on warmed plates, and garnish with red pepper diamonds. Serve immediately, with spinach flavoured tagliatelle.

Tony Davis

> *"This dish invites real eating."*
>
> Gary Rhodes

Cook's Note

For the red pepper garnish, blanch diamonds of seeded red pepper in boiling water for 1 minute, then refresh in cold water and drain.

Chicken Moroccan-style

6-8 chicken thighs (depending on size)

Stuffing:
30 ml (2 tbsp) chopped coriander
30 ml (2 tbsp) chopped parsley
1 preserved lemon (see note)
10 ml (2 tsp) ground cumin
freshly ground black pepper
8 green olives, stoned
3 cloves garlic
30 ml (2 tbsp) olive oil

Marinade:
large pinch of saffron strands

Sauce:
125 ml (4 fl oz) white wine
15 ml (1 tbsp) chopped coriander
15 ml (1 tbsp) chopped parsley
15 g (½ oz) stoned green olives, cut into slivers
few slivers of preserved lemon rind (see note)
150 ml (¼ pint) double cream
salt and freshly ground pepper
squeeze of lemon juice (optional)

Using sharp kitchen scissors, bone the chicken thighs. Put the bones in a roasting tin and brown in a pre-heated oven at 180°C (350°F) mark 4 for 30-45 minutes.

Meanwhile, put all the stuffing ingredients in a blender or food processor and work until the mixture is well blended. Spread a little of this mixture over the inside of each chicken thigh, roll up and tie loosely if necessary with fine string. Place in a shallow dish.

Steep the saffron strands in 300 ml (½ pint) boiling water for about 10 minutes, then strain the liquid over the chicken and leave to marinate for several hours, turning occasionally.

Remove the chicken from the marinade, wipe dry and place in the roasting tin with the bones; reserve 150 ml (¼ pint) marinade. Roast the chicken in the oven for 25-30 minutes until cooked through and crispy on the outside; increase the heat towards the end of the cooking time if necessary. Discard the bones. Transfer the chicken to a warmed plate; keep warm.

Deglaze the pan with the wine. Add the reserved marinade and allow to bubble over a medium heat until syrupy. Strain if necessary, then add the herbs, olives, preserved lemon rind and a little cream. Simmer until rich and creamy. Check the seasoning and add a little lemon juice if preferred.

To serve, slice the chicken. Pour a pool of sauce on to each serving plate and arrange the chicken slices on top. Serve immediately.

Sue Longden

"Ooh, that's very yummy."

Angela Rippon

• Ingredients •

To prepare preserved lemons, wash and dry 450 g (1 lb) unwaxed lemons, then cut lengthwise into quarters, leaving them attached at the base. Sprinkle 30-45 ml (2-3 tbsp) salt over the insides. Reshape and pack into a small sterilized jar. Fill to the brim with cooled boiled water, seal and store in a cool place for about 3 weeks.

Cook's Note

Do use free-range chicken for this and don't be tempted to use chicken breasts, because they haven't the succulency to carry this robustly flavoured sauce. The deliciously perfumed blend of flavourings is inspired by a Moroccan tajine. It includes preserved lemon – a Moroccan speciality – which is easy to prepare.

Stuffed Breast of Chicken in Filo Pastry

Served with a Wild Mushroom Sauce

4 chicken breasts (preferably free-range or corn-fed)
4 sheets of filo pastry
125 g (4 oz) butter, melted
1 egg, beaten, to glaze

Mousse:
125 g (4 oz) boneless chicken breast or thigh meat
75 g (3 oz) spinach leaves
150 ml (¼ pint) double cream
freshly grated nutmeg, to taste
salt and freshly ground pepper
15 g (½ oz) butter
350-450 g (¾-1 lb) wild mushrooms, eg oyster, shiitake

Sauce:
1.2 litres (2 pints) good homemade chicken stock
Madeira, to taste
wild mushrooms(reserved from mousse)
25-50 g (1-2 oz) butter

Cook's Note

Take great care when making the mousse that you keep everything as cold as possible. I prefer to use raw spinach as you get a better colour, but blanch it first if you prefer. You must keep the filo pastry covered with a damp cloth until you are ready to use it or it will dry out.

First prepare the mousse. Put the chicken and spinach in a food processor and work until smooth. Pass through a sieve, chill, then add the cream, nutmeg and seasoning. Heat the butter in a pan and sauté the mushrooms for no longer than 1 minute. Set aside three quarters of them for the sauce.

Open out the chicken breasts as flat as possible. Season, then add a spoonful of mousse together with some sautéed mushrooms. Carefully close the chicken breasts and wrap securely in foil. Bring the stock to the boil in a large pan. Add the chicken and poach for 10 minutes. Remove from the stock and leave to cool, then unwrap. Reduce the stock and reserve.

Brush a sheet of filo pastry with melted butter and fold in half. Brush the top again with butter. Place a chicken breast in the centre and wrap the filo around, folding in the ends, to make a parcel. Repeat with the remaining filo and chicken.

Brush the filo parcels with beaten egg and place on a well buttered baking tray. Cook in a preheated oven at 190°C (375°F) mark 5 for 25 minutes. Just before you serve, add the Madeira to the chicken stock, and check seasoning. Add the remaining mushrooms and poach briefly, then strain.

Arrange the filo parcels on individual plates with the mushrooms. Whisk the butter into the stock in pieces; serve separately as a sauce.

Louise Solden

Chicken in Vermouth

With Leek and Watercress Sauce

4 chicken breasts
175 g (6 oz) button mushrooms, finely chopped
2 shallots, finely chopped
2 leeks, finely chopped
50 ml (2 fl oz) dry vermouth
salt and freshly ground black pepper
50 g (2 oz) butter
small bunch of watercress sprigs
120 ml (4 fl oz) chicken stock
175 ml (6 fl oz) double cream, or to taste

Cook's Note

You must use double cream rather than single otherwise the sauce will curdle when you boil it. Remember to use the green part of the leek for the sauce to strengthen the colour from the watercress.

Place each chicken breast on a square of foil large enough to make a parcel. Sprinkle small amounts of chopped mushroom, shallot and leek over each chicken breast. Pour about 5 ml (1 tsp) vermouth over each chicken breast and season with salt and pepper. Fold the edges of the foil up over the chicken to make a parcel and seal well. Place on a wire rack standing over a roasting tin half-filled with warm water and bake in a preheated oven at 180°C (350°F) mark 4, for 25-30 minutes until tender.

Meanwhile, melt the butter in a frying pan. Add the remaining chopped vegetables with the watercress, reserving a few sprigs for garnish. Sweat gently until soft and well cooked. Add the remaining vermouth and reduce. Add the chicken stock and bring to the boil. Transfer the mixture to a blender and whiz until fairly smooth. Pass through a sieve into a clean frying pan. Add the cream (in moderation), warm through and reserve until required.

Unwrap the chicken parcels, discarding all chopped vegetables, and place the chicken breasts on warmed plates. Pour some sauce over and around each one and garnish with sprigs of watercress. Serve at once with mangetouts tossed in butter and black pepper, and minted new potatoes.

Kieran McBride

Piquant Chicken

with Coriander and Lime Sauces

finely grated rind and juice of 2 limes
2 cloves garlic, crushed
50 g (2 oz) unsalted butter
10 ml (2 tsp) ground coriander
4 chicken breast fillets
salt and freshly ground black pepper

Coriander Sauce:
125 ml (4 fl oz) full-cream milk
225 g (8 oz) block creamed coconut
225 g (8 oz) fresh coriander leaves, finely chopped
125 ml (4 fl oz) double cream

Lime Sauce:
finely grated rind and juice of 6 limes
5 ml (1 tsp) light soft brown sugar

Mix the lime rind and juice with the garlic, butter and coriander; set aside. Remove any sinews from the chicken. Lay out each chicken breast flat, cover with greaseproof paper and beat lightly to flatten, ensuring that the flesh is not broken. Spread both sides of each chicken breast with the flavoured butter, then roll up and wrap tightly in foil, so that none of the juices may escape. Chill in the refrigerator for 30 minutes, then cook in a preheated oven at 190°C (375°F) mark 5 for 40 minutes.

Meanwhile prepare the sauces. For the coriander sauce, place the milk and creamed coconut in a saucepan and heat gently, stirring, until all of the coconut is dissolved. Add the coriander and cook very gently, stirring frequently, for 10 minutes. Purée the sauce in a blender or food processor, then stir in the cream and heat through gently.

For the lime sauce, heat the lime juice and grated rind with the sugar. Unwrap the chicken and add the pan juices to the lime sauce. Reduce to a glaze.

Place the chicken on individual plates, spoon over the lime sauce to glaze and serve with the coriander sauce, spiced rice and French beans.

Tim Robinson

SUPREMES OF CHICKEN

WITH CRAB AND GINGER

30 ml (2 tbsp) olive oil
10 ml (2 tsp) grated fresh ginger
175 g (6 oz) cooked crabmeat
90 ml (6 tbsp) brandy
4 even-sized chicken breasts
125 g (4 oz) butter
2 spring onions, shredded
salt and freshly ground pepper
150 ml (¼ pint) double cream

Heat half the oil in a small pan and sweat the ginger for 1 minute, without browning. Add the crabmeat and cook for 2 minutes. Add 30 ml (2 tbsp) brandy; cook for 1 minute. Season well and leave to cool.

With a small sharp knife, cut a pocket in each chicken breast. Fill with the crabmeat mixture and secure with cocktail sticks, if necessary to ensure the filling stays in. Heat the remaining oil and half of the butter in a frying pan and sear the chicken breasts on both sides. Transfer each one to a piece of foil, season and top with a spring onion shred. Wrap the foil around the chicken and seal.

Place the foil parcels in a preheated oven at 200°C (400°F) mark 6 for 15 minutes or until the chicken is tender. Leave in the sealed parcels for 5 minutes.

Meanwhile make the sauce. Heat the remaining brandy in the butter used for searing, then gradually whisk in the cream. Whisk in the remaining butter, a piece at a time, then season.

To serve unwrap the parcels and transfer the chicken breasts to serving plates. Spoon over the sauce and garnish with the remaining shredded spring onion.

Johnny Wong

CHICKEN BREAST STUFFED WITH A PISTACHIO MOUSSELINE

SERVED WITH TWO SAUCES

4 chicken breasts (preferably corn-fed), skinned
½ egg white
15 ml (1 tbsp) double cream
30 ml (2 tbsp) pistachio nuts

Mango Sauce:
1 ripe mango
knob of butter
1 shallot, chopped
150 ml (¼ pint) full-bodied white wine
15 ml-30 ml (1-2 tbsp) double cream
salt and freshly ground pepper

Watercress Sauce:
150 ml (¼ pint) single cream
1 bunch of watercress

To Garnish:
lime slices
tarragon sprigs

• COOK'S NOTE •

Stuffings can often be rather bland for my liking but this one with pistachios marries well with the chicken. If you prefer, leave on the chicken skin and pop under the grill for the last five minutes of cooking to give a crisp finish. The advantage of this dish is that the sauces can be made a couple of hours in advance and reduced a few minutes before serving.

For the mango sauce, peel the mango and chop roughly, discarding the stone. Place in a blender, whiz until smooth, then pass through a sieve. Melt the butter in a pan and sauté the shallot until softened. Deglaze the pan with the white wine and simmer until reduced by half. Add the mango purée and stir well. Add the cream and reduce until slightly thickened. If it thickens too much, add a dash more wine. Season with salt and pepper.

For the watercress sauce, put the cream, 30 ml (2 tbsp) water and the watercress in a pan. Simmer gently for 8 minutes, then leave to cool for a few minutes. Whiz in a blender until smooth, then pass through a sieve. Return the sauce to the pan, reduce until slightly thickened and season with salt and pepper.

Trim the chicken breasts and put the trimmings in a blender with the egg white, cream and pistachios. Whiz for a few seconds, leaving the nuts slightly crunchy. Lay the chicken breasts out and spread the underside with mousseline mixture. Roll up from one end to the other, wrap each one in foil and place on a baking tray. Bake in a preheated oven at 220°C (425°F) mark 7, for 15-20 minutes.

Unwrap each foil parcel, and slice the rolled chicken breasts across into 4-5 pieces. Arrange on warmed serving plates and pour the sauces on either side. Garnish with lime slices and tarragon sprigs. Serve immediately, with vegetables of your choice.

Richard Sutton

Right: *Chicken Breast Stuffed with a Pistachio Mousseline*

SALT-ROAST DUCK

WITH CARAMEL SAUCE

2 duck breasts, with skin
freshly ground black pepper
1.4 kg (3 lb) coarse sea salt
6 egg whites
freshly ground pepper

Caramel Sauce:
45 ml (3 tbsp) sugar
250 ml (8 fl oz) red wine vinegar
300 ml (½ pint) strong duck stock
150 ml (¼ pint) double cream

Score shallow crosses in the skin of the duck breasts with a sharp knife. Heat a heavy-based frying pan and brown the duck breasts, one at a time, skin side down, for 3 minutes, then remove. Sprinkle the duck breasts with pepper and reform into their original shape by tying at each end with string.

Mix the sea salt with the egg whites and put a thin layer in the base of two 1 kg (2 lb) loaf tins. Put a duck breast in each tin and cover completely with more salt. Roast immediately in a preheated oven at 230°C (450°F) mark 8 for 17 minutes. Remove and let stand for 10 minutes.

Meanwhile, make the caramel sauce. In a deep saucepan, dissolve the sugar in the vinegar over low heat, then increase the heat and cook to a caramel, about 10 minutes. Mix in the stock and bring to the boil. Add the cream, but do not stir! Boil vigorously for 5-8 minutes, or until the sauce is boiling with small bubbles; the stronger your stock, the quicker this will happen. Stir gently and remove from the heat. Season with a little pepper. Keep warm over a saucepan of hot water.

Break open the salt crust and take out the duck breasts. Wipe off the salt with paper towels, remove the duck skin, then thinly slice the duck breasts and serve with pepper.

Orlando Murrin

COOK'S NOTE

This is a remarkable and totally reliable way of cooking duck to perfection. The salt draws out all the fat from the meat, and the flavour is magical – not at all salty. The glistening caramel sauce is richly flavoured – not at all of vinegar – and quite unlike any other! Buy a whole duck and use the rest of the carcass to make the stock for the sauce.

> *"That is clever, lovely combination."*
>
> Sue Lawley

GUINEA FOWL IN AN ORANGE SAUCE

WITH CHESTNUTS

4 guinea fowl joints, skinned
salt and freshly ground black pepper
30 ml (2 tbsp) oil
25 g (1 oz) butter
200 g (7 oz) button onions
200 ml (7 fl oz) stock
150 ml (¼ pint) white wine
finely pared rind and juice of 1 orange
15 ml (1 tbsp) redcurrant jelly
30 ml (2 tbsp) flour
425 g (15 oz) can unsweetened chestnuts, drained

Season the guinea fowl joints with salt and pepper. Heat the oil and half of the butter in a frying pan and add the guinea fowl joints. Turn until evenly browned, then transfer them to a casserole dish, using a slotted spoon.

Brown the button onions in the fat remaining in the frying pan, then add them to the casserole dish.

Mix together the stock, wine and orange juice. Add the redcurrant jelly and stir to dissolve. Gradually stir this mixture into the flour.

Pour the stock mixture into the frying pan and cook, stirring, until thickened and smooth, then pour over the guinea fowl and onions. Add half of the chestnuts with the orange rind, cut into strips. Adjust the seasoning and cook in a preheated oven at 180°C (350°F) mark 4 for about 1 hour.

Heat the remaining chestnuts slowly in the rest of the butter. Serve the guinea fowl in the sauce, garnished with the chestnuts and accompanied by vegetables.

Anne May

STEAMED GUINEA FOWL

WITH WILD MUSHROOMS

4 guinea fowl chicks
8 thyme sprigs
salt and freshly ground white pepper
4 fresh or dried juniper berries
20 ml (4 tsp) each brandy, port and Madeira

Sauce:
50 g (2 oz) clarified butter
30 ml (2 tbsp) diced shallot
15 ml (1 tbsp) diced carrot
15 ml (1 tbsp) diced celery
3 cloves garlic, split
5 thyme sprigs
2.5 ml (½ tsp) white pepper
15 ml (1 tbsp) brandy
120 ml (4 fl oz) dry white wine
600 ml (1 pint) veal stock
150 ml (¼ pint) water
15 ml (1 tbsp) tomato purée
½ bay leaf
10 ml (2 tsp) cream

To Serve:
10 pencil-thin leeks, halved
8 shallots, chopped
225 g (8 oz) chanterelle mushrooms
225 g (8 oz) trumpet mushrooms
knob of butter
4 ravioli of wild mushrooms (optional)

Cut the backbone from the birds and reserve for stock. Cut off the wing tips and leg tips. Remove the wishbones and reserve. Place a sprig of thyme between the skin and breast of each bird. Season the bird cavities and add the juniper berries and 15 ml (1 tsp) each of brandy, port and Madeira. Put each bird in a roasting bag, expel the air and secure with a knot. Place in a pan of boiling water and steam for 20 minutes. Remove and let to rest for 5 minutes.

Meanwhile, make the sauce. Heat the butter in a heavy-based pan and brown the guinea fowl bones. Add the shallot, carrot and celery, 1 split clove garlic, 1 thyme sprig and pepper. Cook for 2 minutes, then deglaze with the brandy. Cook for 2 minutes, then add the wine and reduce by half. Add the stock, water, tomato purée, bay leaf, 4 thyme sprigs and the remaining garlic. Bring to the boil, skim well and simmer for 10 minutes. Pass the sauce through a sieve lined with a double thickness of muslin. Return to the cleaned pan, bring back to the boil and reduce by half. Add the cream and seasoning. Whisk lightly and keep warm.

Blanch the leeks in boiling salted water for 1 minute; keep warm. Quickly sauté the shallots and mushrooms in a knob of butter to soften.

Remove the birds from the roasting bags. Carve off the breasts and legs and discard the skin. Remove the thigh bones. Arrange the guinea fowl breasts and legs on warmed serving plates. Arrange the leeks and mushrooms around the meat. Spoon the sauce over the meat. Serve with homemade ravioli with a mushroom filling if desired.

Scott Findlay

Right: *Steamed Guinea Fowl with Wild Mushrooms*

Grilled Breast of Duck

in Red Wine Sauce

4 duck breasts, each about 175 g (6 oz), boned (carcasses reserved)
15 ml (1 tbsp) each finely chopped basil, rosemary, sage and thyme

Sauce:
15 ml (1 tbsp) butter
15 ml (1 tbsp) oil
150 ml (¼ pint) red wine
2 shallots, chopped
15 ml (1 tbsp) tomato purée
30 ml (2 tbsp) brandy
600 ml (1 pint) rich brown poultry stock
beurre manié, ie 15 ml (1 tbsp) butter blended with 15 ml (1 tbsp) flour

To Garnish:
thyme sprigs

"If you got that in a restaurant you would feel you had done well."

Andrew Neil

To prepare the sauce, chop the duck carcasses into small pieces. Heat the butter and oil in a large pan and add the duck bones. Cook, turning occasionally, until browned. Remove the excess fat from the pan, then deglaze with the red wine, stirring to scrape up the sediment.

Add the chopped shallots, tomato purée and brandy, then flambé. When the flames subside, add the brown poultry stock. Boil to reduce by half. Strain through a sieve lined with a double thickness of muslin, correct the seasoning and return to the cleaned pan. Thicken the sauce with beurre manié, adding it a little at a time, until the sauce reaches a coating consistency. Set aside.

To prepare the duck breasts, remove the tendon from each one. Press the chopped herbs on to the breasts and cook under a preheated grill for about 4 minutes each side until browned on the outside, but still rare in the middle. Leave to rest for 5-10 minutes before carving.

Pour a pool of sauce on to each warmed plate and arrange the duck on top. Garnish with thyme sprigs. Serve with Potato and Mushroom Cakes (page 120), and seasonal vegetables.

Martha Spencer

Left: *Grilled Breast of Duck in Red Wine Sauce*

Barbary Duck Breast

with Honey and Thyme

30 ml (2 tbsp) oil or butter
4 Barbary duck breasts
4 shallots, diced
juice of 1 lemon
10 ml (2 tsp) chopped thyme
30 ml (2 tbsp) clear honey
10 ml (2 tsp) soy sauce
finely pared rind of ½ lemon, thinly sliced

Heat the oil or butter in a large heavy-based frying pan, add the duck breasts skin-side down and fry over a moderate heat for 6-8 minutes. Turn the duck breasts over, lower the heat and cook until almost tender.

Add the shallots, lemon juice and thyme. Bring to the boil, add the honey and soy sauce and cook for 2 minutes.

"This is a good honest dish."

Loyd

Remove the duck breasts and strain off the fat from the pan. Add the lemon rind shreds to the juices remaining in the pan and bring back to the boil. Meanwhile slice the duck breasts and arrange them on individual plates. Pour the pan juices and lemon rind over the duck and serve immediately, with seasonal vegetables.

Robin Machin

Quails with Couscous

15 ml (1 tbsp) olive oil or melted butter
salt and freshly ground black pepper
225 g (8 oz) couscous
30-45 ml (2-3 tbsp) pine nuts, toasted
50-75 g (2-3 oz) large plump raisins, soaked in Armagnac
4 pairs quails
8 rashers bacon
120 ml (4 fl oz) little red wine (approximately)

To Garnish:
few coriander or parsley sprigs

Put 300 ml (½ pint) water and 15 ml (1 tbsp) olive oil or butter in a large saucepan. Add a pinch of salt and bring to the boil. Remove from the heat, add the couscous, stir and leave to swell for 15 minutes. Stir again and add the pine nuts and raisins. Stuff the quails with some of the couscous mixture, and secure with cocktail sticks.

Cover each quail with a rasher of bacon and place in a roasting dish. Pour in the red wine and season with salt and pepper. Bake in a preheated oven at 220-230°C (425-450°F) mark 7-8 for 8-10 minutes, until very tender. Keep testing the birds towards the end of cooking; it is essential to avoid overcooking them. Discard the cocktail sticks. Strain the cooking juices.

Reheat the remaining couscous and pile in the centre of a serving dish. Surround with the quails, pour over the cooking juices and garnish with coriander or parsley.

Joan Bunting

Pan-fried Supremes of Quail

with Grapes and a Sauternes Sauce

8 quails
60 ml (4 tbsp) butter
175 g (6 oz) seedless grapes, peeled
150 ml (¼ pint) sauternes wine

Croûtons:
4 slices homemade white bread, each 5 mm (¼ inch) thick
clarified butter, for frying

To Garnish:
4 slices canned 'block' foie gras, each 5 mm (¼ inch) thick
30 ml (2 tbsp) sauternes wine

To prepare the quails, slip your fingers between the skin and flesh, then pull away the skin. Cut against the ridge of the breastbone to loosen the flesh from the bone. Disjoint the wing where it joins the carcass and continue down along the rib cage, pulling flesh from bone as you cut until the meat from one side of the breast separates from the bone in one piece. Repeat on the other side.

To make the croûtons, cut the bread into rounds using a fluted cutter. Heat a 3 mm (⅛ inch) depth of clarified butter in a frying pan and sauté the bread rounds on each side until very lightly browned. Drain on absorbent kitchen paper.

Place the foie gras slices in a covered dish and baste with the sauternes. Ten minutes before serving, set the dish over a pan of barely simmering water, to heat through.

Heat the butter in a sauté pan until it is foaming. Quickly roll the quail supremes in the butter and cook briefly until the flesh springs back with gentle resilience. Transfer the supremes to a warm platter, using a slotted spoon, and cover while making the sauce. Warm the grapes in the butter remaining in the pan, then remove with a slotted spoon. Keep warm with the supremes.

Pour the wine into the sauté pan and reduce quickly over a high heat until the liquid is syrupy. Remove from the heat and check the seasoning, then strain through a muslin-lined sieve.

To serve, arrange the quail supremes and grapes on warmed serving plates. Pour over the sauternes sauce and garnish with the foie gras and croûtons. Serve with vegetables.

Martha Spencer

Martha Spencer – Finalist 1991

Martha is currently using the magnificent backdrop of her home Airlie Castle in Angus to host cookery demonstrations. Even her fellow contestant Sue Lawrence has been known to make appearances! Competition sucess has also been smiling on Martha and she is current holder of the title Sunday Times International Amateur Chef of the Year.

Right: *Pan-fried Supremes of Quail with Grapes and a Sauternes Sauce*

Roasted Breast of Wood Pigeon

with Forest Mushrooms and a Balsamic Vinegar and Port Sauce

3 plump wood pigeons' breasts
20 ml (4 tsp) walnut oil
20 ml (4 tsp) hazelnut oil
10 ml (2 tsp) olive oil
50 g (2 oz) mixed dried forest mushrooms (chanterelles, horn of plenty, ceps)
40 g (1½ oz) butter
1 small onion
10 ml (2 tsp) dried herbs de Provence
60 ml (2 fl oz) balsamic vinegar
175 ml (6 fl oz) port
300 ml (½ pint) game stock
salt and freshly ground black pepper
few fresh chanterelles (if available)

To Serve
Puy Lentils (page 121)

Remove the skin from the pigeon breasts and prick the flesh lightly all over with a fork. Place in a shallow dish and drizzle with 10 ml (2 tsp) each of walnut, hazelnut and olive oil. Turn the pigeon breasts to coat with the oils, cover and leave to marinate in a cool place overnight.

Meanwhile put the dried mushrooms in a small bowl, add cold water to cover and leave to soak overnight.

Melt 15 g (½ oz) of the butter in a frying pan and seal the pigeon breasts over a very high heat for 1 minute each side. Transfer to a baking tray and cover with foil.

To make the sauce, chop the onion very finely. Heat 10 ml (2 tsp) each of hazelnut and walnut oil with 15 g (½ oz) butter in a pan. Add the onion and cook for 2 minutes until softened. Drain the soaked mushrooms, reserving the liquid, and add to the pan with the herbs. Fry, stirring, for 5 minutes.

Add the vinegar to the pan and boil vigorously until the mixture is almost dry. Add the port and boil to reduce by half. Add the stock and reserved mushroom liquor, and reduce by one third. Season with salt and pepper to taste; keep warm.

Cook the pigeon breasts in a preheated oven at 220°C (425°F) mark 7 for 5 minutes. Remove from the oven and leave to rest covered with foil for 5 minutes. Meanwhile sauté the fresh mushrooms in a little butter until tender.

To serve, thinly slice the pigeon breasts and arrange on warmed serving plates on a pile of lentils. Garnish with the sautéed chanterelles and surround with the sauce.

Amanda Dawson

Cook's Note

For this recipe, choose plump wood pigeons. Carefully remove the whole breasts and use the rest of the carcasses to make the stock. You will need to marinate the pigeon (and soak the mushrooms) overnight.

Wood Pigeons with Wild and Brown Rice Stuffing

and Juniper and Port Sauce

4 wood pigeons

Stuffing:
25 g (1 oz) wild rice
175 g (6 oz) brown rice
25 g (1 oz) butter
2 rashers streaky bacon, finely chopped
1 shallot, finely chopped
grated rind of 1 orange
25 g (1 oz) walnuts, skinned and finely chopped
salt and freshly ground pepper
15-30 ml (1-2 tbsp) chopped coriander leaves

Sauce:
30 ml (2 tbsp) oil
50 g (2 oz) butter
1 onion, chopped
4 juniper berries, crushed
few thyme sprigs
300 ml (½ pint) homemade stock
125 ml (4 fl oz) port
15 ml (1 tbsp) redcurrant jelly
salt and freshly ground pepper

"Very, very understated juniper and port sauce."

Loyd

Wash and dry the pigeons. For the stuffing, wash the wild rice and brown rice separately. Cook the wild rice in boiling salted water in a covered pan for 30 minutes or until tender; drain. Heat the butter in a pan, add the bacon and shallot and sauté until the shallot is softened. Add the brown rice and cook, stirring continuously, until the rice becomes translucent. Add 275 ml (9 fl oz) water and bring to the boil, then simmer covered for 20-25 minutes or until the rice is tender. Add the orange rind, wild rice, walnuts, seasoning and coriander.

To make the sauce, heat the oil and half of the butter in a pan and quickly seal the pigeons, then remove. Add the onion to the pan and fry until softened. Stir in the juniper berries, thyme, stock and port and bring to the boil. Simmer until the sauce has reduced by half. Strain the sauce into a clean pan. Add the redcurrant jelly and stir over moderate heat until the jelly has melted. Beat in the remaining butter, a little at a time, and adjust the seasoning. Keep warm.

Stuff the pigeons with the rice mixture and truss with fine string. Place in a roasting dish. Cook in a preheated oven at 220°C, (425°F) mark 7 for 20-25 minutes or until tender. Remove string. Place the pigeons on warmed plates and spoon over the sauce to serve.

Amita Baldock

Pigeon Breasts on Perfumed Cabbage

4 young pigeons
60 ml (4 tbsp) olive, hazelnut or walnut oil
½ bottle good red wine
5 ml (1 tsp) redcurrant jelly
2 cloves garlic
8-10 juniper berries
pinch of salt
700 g (1½ lb) white cabbage, cored and finely shredded
25 g (1 oz) chilled butter
30 ml (2 tbsp) double cream
30 ml (2 tbsp) chopped chervil or flat-leaved parsley

Garnish:
redcurrants or parsley sprigs

Cook's Note

I like to get ahead of myself on this one and always have stock on hand in the freezer rather than have to boil it up in a hurry.

Remove the breasts from the pigeons, reserving the carcasses. Marinate in the oil, turning from time to time, for about 2 hours. Chop the pigeon carcasses and brown in a large greased pan. Add water to cover and simmer steadily for 1½ hours. Strain and simmer to reduce to about 300 ml (½ pint). Add the wine and redcurrant jelly and simmer until reduced to about one third. Set aside.

Pound the garlic and juniper berries with a pinch of salt to a paste, using a pestle and mortar.

Grease a frying pan and sear the pigeon breasts on both sides. Transfer to a greased baking tray and cook in a preheated oven at 230°C (450°F) mark 8 for 6 minutes. Cover the pigeons with foil and leave to rest while you cook the cabbage.

Heat a wok or frying pan and melt half of the butter. Add the garlic and juniper paste and stir round to loosen for a few seconds, then increase the heat and add the cabbage. Cook, stirring constantly, until it begins to lose its raw state. Add the cream and lower the heat.

Reheat the red wine sauce and slice the pigeon breasts lengthwise, into thin pink teardrops. Add the chervil or parsley to the cabbage, toss well and place a small mound in the centre of each plate. Arrange the pigeon slices around the cabbage. Add the remaining butter to the red wine sauce in tiny pieces, shaking the pan as you do so, to thicken the sauce and give it gloss. Trickle the sauce around the cabbage and garnish with redcurrants or parsley to serve.

Angela Jaques

Pheasant Breast with Chanterelles and Grapes

on a Potato Pancake

4 pheasant breasts
90 g (3½ oz) chanterelles or other wild mushrooms
150 g (5 oz) red grapes
salt and freshly ground black pepper
15 ml (1 tbsp) oil
40 g (1½ oz) butter, chilled and diced
85 ml (6 tbsp) white wine
300 ml (½ pint) pheasant stock

Potato Cakes:
350 g (12 oz) large potatoes
50 g (2 oz) clarified butter

To Serve:
chervil sprigs, to garnish
few drops of truffle oil (optional)

Trim the pheasant breasts. Clean the mushrooms thoroughly. Halve and deseed the grapes.

To make the potato cakes, peel and thinly slice the potatoes, then mix with the clarified butter. Season with salt and pepper. Form into 4 potato cakes, each 10 cm (4 inches) across and 5 mm (¼ inch) deep. Fry the potato cakes in a heavy-based pan, pressing down firmly, until crisp and golden brown on both sides; keep warm.

Heat 15 ml (1 tbsp) oil and 25 g (1 oz) butter in another pan, add the pheasant breasts and fry briefly over a high heat until well browned. Turn and repeat on the other side. The cooked pheasant breasts must remain pink inside otherwise they become dry. Using a slotted spoon, transfer to an ovenproof dish.

Add the mushrooms to the pan and sauté gently, adding the grapes when the mushrooms are almost cooked. Add to the pheasant and keep warm. Drain off the oil from the pan.

Deglaze the pan with the white wine. Reduce until almost completely evaporated, then add the stock. Boil rapidly to reduce until the sauce starts to thicken. Strain through a muslin-lined sieve into a clean pan and reheat.

Reheat the pheasant, mushrooms and grapes in a preheated oven at 220°C (425°F) mark 7 for 1 minute. Meanwhile whisk the remaining 15 g (½ oz) butter into the sauce, a piece at a time.

Place a potato cake on the centre of each warmed serving plate. Slice the pheasant and arrange on top of the potato cakes. Arrange the mushrooms, grapes and sprigs of chervil around the pheasant and moisten with the sauce. Sprinkle the pheasant with a drop of truffle oil to add richness to the dish, if desired. Serve immediately, accompanied by vegetable purées, such as carrot and potato, and parsnip purées.

Ross Burden

Cook's Note

Use the carcasses from the pheasants to make a well-flavoured stock.

Pheasant Pie

with Potato Pastry

1 cock pheasant
25 g (1 oz) butter
100 g (4 oz) British smoked bacon rashers, derinded and chopped
1 onion, sliced
1 Bramley apple, peeled, cored and sliced
450 ml (¾ pint) cider
bouquet garni, ie sprig each of marjoram, parsley and thyme
4 cloves
salt and freshly ground black pepper
squeeze of lemon juice

Potato Pastry:
175 g (6 oz) self-raising flour
125 g (4 oz) butter
175 g (6 oz) cold mashed potato
beaten egg for brushing

Cook's Note

This pastry is deliciously short and well worth the effort. You can of course use cold leftover potatoes if you have some.

Right: *Pheasant Pie*

Carefully remove the breasts and legs from the pheasant. (Use the rest of the meat and carcass to make stock for another dish.) Slice the meat, discarding the bones.

Heat the butter in a heavy-based pan and fry the bacon and onion until golden. Add the pheasant slices together with the apple slices and fry turning for a few minutes. Add the cider, bouquet garni, cloves, seasoning and lemon juice. Cover and cook for 45 minutes to 1 hour until the pheasant is tender. Discard the bouquet garni.

Meanwhile make the potato pastry. Sift the flour into a bowl, rub in the butter until the mixture resembles breadcrumbs, then add the mashed potato to bind the pastry. Wrap and leave to rest in the refrigerator for about 15 minutes.

Transfer the pheasant mixture to a pie dish. Roll out the pastry on a lightly floured surface to make a pie lid. Moisten the rim of the pie dish and position the pastry over the meat. Decorate the top of the pie with shapes cut from the trimmings. Brush with beaten egg and cook in a preheated oven at 200°C (400°F) mark 6 for 25 minutes. Serve immediately, with vegetables.

Pheasant Stock: Make this from the leftover pheasant carcass. Put the pheasant carcass in a saucepan or pressure cooker with water to cover and flavouring ingredients – 1 onion, 1 leek, 1 carrot, chopped; 1 clove garlic, crushed; and seasoning. Bring to the boil and cook for 1½ hours, or 30 minutes in a pressure cooker. Strain before using as required.

Linda Yewdall

Venison with a Juniper and Port Sauce

25 g (1 oz) butter
15 ml (1 tbsp) walnut oil
2 fillets of venison, each about 225 g (8 oz), taken from the saddle

Sauce:
300 ml (½ pint) game stock
150 ml (¼ pint) port
12 juniper berries, crushed
50 g (2 oz) unsalted butter, in pieces
salt and freshly ground black pepper

First make the sauce. Put the game stock, port and juniper berries in a saucepan and simmer until reduced by half. Off the heat, whisk in the unsalted butter, a piece at a time. Pass through a muslin-lined sieve into a bowl and season with salt and freshly ground black pepper to taste.

In a roasting tin, heat the butter with the walnut oil. Add the venison fillets and quickly sear all over on a high heat. Transfer to a preheated oven at 200°C (400°F) mark 6 and roast for 10 minutes. Cover with foil and leave to rest for a few minutes in a warm place, then carve into fine slices.

To serve, arrange a circle of venison slices on each serving plate and surround with the sauce. Serve with asparagus, and other vegetable accompaniments.

Chris Duckham

Venison with a Sloe Gin and Bramble Sauce

450 g (1 lb) fillet of venison
olive oil, for brushing

Marinade:
300 ml (½ pint) red wine
30 ml (2 tbsp) olive oil
salt and freshly ground pepper

Sauce:
450 ml (¾ pint) demi glace (see below)
75-90 ml (5-6 tbsp) blackberry juice
45 ml (3 tbsp) red wine
5 juniper berries, crushed
4 pink peppercorns, crushed
45 ml (3 tbsp) sloe gin
125 g (4 oz) blackberries
knob of butter

To Garnish:
thyme sprigs

"It's a poetic mixture."

Myrtle Allen

Place the venison in a shallow dish. Mix together the ingredients for the marinade and pour over the venison. Leave to marinate for 1½ hours.

Remove the venison from the marinade, pat dry and brush with olive oil. Roast in a preheated oven at 200°C (400°F) mark 6 for 15-20 minutes.

Meanwhile, prepare the sauce. Put the demi glace, blackberry juice, wine, juniper berries and pink peppercorns in a saucepan and bring to the boil. Simmer until reduced by a third; the sauce should be thick enough to coat the back of a spoon. Add the sloe gin and transfer to a bain marie, or a heatproof bowl over a pan of hot but not boiling water. Add the blackberries and leave to cook gently for 10 minutes, then remove with a slotted spoon.

Place a small mound of blackberries in the centre of each plate. Whisk the knob of butter into the sauce and season with salt and pepper to taste. Cut the venison into 3mm (⅛ inch) slices and arrange overlapping around the blackberries. Spoon the sauce over the venison slices and serve immediately, garnished with thyme and accompanied by vegetables.

Demi glace: Measure 1 litre (1¾ pints) well-flavoured brown veal stock into a clean pan. Whisk in 3 egg whites and simmer for 10 minutes, then strain through a muslin-lined stainless steel sieve into another pan. Tie 15 ml (1 tbsp) dried Provençal herbs in a muslin bouquet, add to the beautifully clear stock and simmer until reduced to 450 ml (¾ pint).

Jo Eitel

Right: *Venison with a Sloe Gin and Bramble Sauce*

Venison in a Damson Brandy Sauce

4 venison fillets, each weighing about 175 g (6 oz)
15 ml (1 tbsp) olive oil

Marinade:
30 ml (2 tbsp) hazelnut oil
salt and freshly ground black pepper
fresh bouquet garni, eg sprigs of parsley, thyme, bay leaf
2 glasses good red wine
1 carrot, chopped
1 small onion, chopped
1 celery stick, chopped
3 juniper berries

Sauce:
450 ml (¾ pint) venison stock
225 g (8 oz) damsons
1 cinnamon stick
30 ml (2 tbsp) red wine vinegar
75 ml (3 fl oz) damson brandy
25 g (1 oz) chilled butter, diced

"Spinach and venison are wonderful together."

Caroline Waldegrave

Brush the venison fillets with the hazelnut oil, then season with salt and pepper. Place in a shallow container with all the other marinade ingredients, cover and leave to marinate for 1-2 hours. Meanwhile prepare the sauce. Simmer the venison stock in a saucepan until reduced by about half.

Set aside 8 damsons for garnish. Put the rest in a saucepan with the cinnamon stick and 15 ml (1 tbsp) water. Cook until quite soft. Discard the cinnamon and remove the damson stones. Purée the damsons in a blender or food processor, then pass through a sieve.

Heat the wine vinegar in a saucepan until it has almost evaporated, then add the stock, damson purée and damson brandy. Add the 8 reserved damson and heat through gently until softened; lift out with a slotted spoon, then carefully remove the stones, retaining the shape of the fruit. Reserve for garnish. Season the sauce and simmer until reduced and thick enough to coat the back of a spoon.

Remove the venison from the marinade and pat dry with absorbent kitchen paper. Reserve the marinade. Heat the oil in a frying pan and seal the venison for about 1 minute on each side.

Transfer the venison to an ovenproof dish, pour over the marinade and cook in a preheated oven at 190°C (375°F) mark 5 for 10-12 minutes. Meanwhile, whisk the butter into the sauce, a piece at a time.

To serve, cut the venison into 1 cm (½ inch) thick medallions. Arrange in an overlapping circle on each serving plate. Spoon the sauce over the meat and garnish with the damsons.

Damson Brandy: Put 600 ml (1 pint) brandy, 450 g (1 lb) damsons and 225 g (8 oz) sugar in a sterilized wide-necked jar, seal and leave in a dark place for 8 weeks to mature. Strain off the fruit and eat separately. Bottle the damson brandy.

If damson brandy is unobtainable, substitute 75 ml (3 fl oz) brandy and 10 ml (2 tsp) brown sugar, and increase the quantity of damsons to 300 g (10 oz).

Vera Bloor

"A great success"

Patrick Moore

Cook's Note

I use wild, young venison and my own homemade damson brandy for this recipe.

Venison with Elderberry Jelly and Thyme

2 venison fillets, each about 350 g (12 oz), trimmed
30 ml (2 tbsp) hazelnut oil (approximately)
small handful of thyme sprigs
15 ml (1 tbsp) olive oil
50 g (2 oz) butter
2 glasses (good) red wine
450 ml (¾ pint) venison stock
30 ml (2 tbsp) elderberry jelly
salt and freshly ground pepper

To Garnish:
few elderberries (fresh or frozen)
thyme sprigs

To Serve:
Braised Red Cabbage (page 112)

Brush the venison fillets with hazelnut oil and press thyme sprigs all over them. Cover and leave to marinate for 1-2 hours.

Heat the olive oil and half of the butter in a frying pan, then add the venison. Cook, turning, for about 6 minutes until sealed and browned on all sides.

Transfer to an ovenproof dish and leave to rest in a preheated oven at 150°C (300°F) mark 2 for no longer than 8 minutes.

Meanwhile, add the wine to the frying pan, stirring to deglaze, then reduce to about half of the volume. Add the stock and reduce by about half. Add a few thyme sprigs with the elderberry jelly. Stir well and reduce slightly. Add the remaining butter, in pieces, to give a glossy finish. Check the seasoning. Strain the sauce into a jug.

To serve, cut the venison into 1 cm (½ inch) medallions. Arrange in an overlapping circle on each plate, with the braised red cabbage in the centre. Spoon the sauce around the meat. Garnish with elderberries and thyme sprigs.

Sue Lawrence

Cook's Note

Use farmed, well-hung venison for this dish.

> "I go for that in a big way."
>
> Sue MacGregor

Behind the Scenes...

"Throughout the series our guest chefs have consistently stressed the importance of good shopping. I agree with them: you can't cook really well without great produce. Our contestants have been extraodinarily assiduous in their search for the best raw materials. Friendship with fishmongers, good fellowship with greengrocers, bonhomie with butchers, is a vital and desirable part of the MasterChef formula. No contestant showed more spirit in the search for the best produce than one of 1993's cooks who cooked pigeons that she'd shot herself!"

...Loyd

Rabbit with Wild Mushroom Sauce

5 large shallots
3 cloves garlic
125 g (4 oz) butter
1 thyme sprig
½ bay leaf
12 g (½ oz) dried mushrooms, crushed
400 g (14 oz) white button mushrooms
200 ml (7 fl oz) white wine
100 ml (3½ fl oz) Madeira
300 ml (½ pint) chicken stock
2 saddles of rabbit
150 ml (¼ pint) whipping cream

Left: *Rabbit with Wild Mushroom Sauce*

Finely slice the shallots and garlic. Melt 40 g (1½ oz) of the butter in a pan. Add the shallots and garlic with the thyme, bay leaf and dried mushrooms. Cook until the shallots are opaque.

Meanwhile coarsely slice the button mushrooms. Add to the pan and cook, stirring, until all excess liquid has evaporated.

Add the white wine and reduce by half. Add the Madeira. Pour in the chicken stock, bring to the boil and simmer for 20 minutes. Strain the sauce, then return to the pan and reduce by half.

Meanwhile, heat another 50 g (2 oz) butter in a frying pan and brown the saddles of rabbit quickly on all sides. Remove from the pan, wrap in foil and cook in a preheated oven at 190°C (375°F) mark 5 for 10-15 minutes. Leave to rest in the foil for 5 minutes. To finish the sauce, stir in the cream, then whisk in the remaining 15 g (½ oz) chilled butter, a piece at a time.

Slice the rabbit and arrange on warmed serving plates. Spoon the sauce over the rabbit and serve immediately, with vegetable accompaniments.

Helen Weller

Wild Rabbit in Cider and Rosemary

4 rabbit joints
15 ml (1 tbsp) flour
15 ml (1 tbsp) English mustard powder
30 ml (2 tbsp) sunflower oil
30 ml (2 tbsp) olive oil
knob of butter
1 onion, chopped
150 ml (¼ pint) cider
300 ml (½ pint) rabbit stock
1 rosemary sprig
1 bay leaf
5 ml (1 tsp) brown sugar
salt and freshly ground black pepper
chopped parsley, to garnish

If the joints are from an older rabbit, remove the sinews in the hind legs. Toss the rabbit joints in the flour and mustard powder (it is easiest to do this in a plastic bag). Reserve the excess flour mixture.

Heat the sunflower and olive oils in a flameproof casserole, add the rabbit joints and seal on all sides. Remove the rabbit and set aside. Add the butter to the casserole dish, add the onion and sweat until softened. Stir in the remaining flour and cook, stirring, for 1-2 minutes. Gradually stir in the cider, followed by the stock. Bring to the boil, adding the rosemary, bay leaf, seasoning and brown sugar. Return the rabbit joints to the casserole, cover and cook in a preheated oven at 160°C (325°F) mark 3 for 1¼-1½ hours.

Serve garnished with parsley and accompanied by prune-stuffed baked apples, puréed parsnips and mangetouts.

Sarah Marsh

VEGETARIAN DISHES

VEGETABLE, FRUIT AND NUT SAMOSAS

2 large carrots, sliced
1 orange
30 ml (2 tbsp) olive oil
1 medium onion, chopped
5 ml (1 tsp) ground coriander
5 ml (1 tsp) ground cinnamon
5 ml (1 tsp) ground cardamom seeds
2 large courgettes, sliced
50 g (2 oz) raisins
25 g (1 oz) chopped hazelnuts
25 g (1 oz) chopped walnuts
15 ml (1 tbsp) desiccated coconut
25-50 g (1-2 oz) ground almonds
90 ml (3 fl oz) orange juice (approximately)
salt and freshly ground black pepper
4 sheets of filo pastry
melted butter for brushing
15-30 ml (1-2 tbsp) flaked almonds

Citrus Sauce:
1 large orange
juice of 1 lemon
300 ml (½ pint) fresh orange juice
2.5 ml (½ tsp) ground cardamom seeds
2.5 ml (½ tsp) ground cinnamon
sugar, to taste
15 ml (1 tbsp) Cointreau (optional)
1.25 ml (¼ tsp) arrowroot

To Garnish:
finely shredded orange and lemon rind
chopped pistachio nuts
coriander leaves

Steam the carrots for about 5 minutes; they should still be crisp. Peel and segment the orange, discarding all pith and pips; chop the flesh.

Heat the oil in a saucepan and fry the onion for a few minutes. Add the spices and heat through. Add the steamed carrots and courgettes and cook for 1 minute, stirring continuously.

Add the orange, raisins, chopped nuts, coconut, ground almonds and orange juice. The mixture should hold together; if it is too dry add a little more juice; if too liquid add more ground almonds. Stir well to thoroughly mix all the ingredients together, then season with salt and pepper to taste.

Cut each sheet of filo pastry into quarters, then fold each quarter in half lengthwise to give 4 strips. Brush each strip with melted butter. Lay 4 filo pastry strips over each of 4 ramekins, crossing them to form a Union Jack pattern and allowing the strips to overlap the edge. Push the pastry down inside the ramekins to line the base and sides. Fill each well with samosa mixture and fold the pastry flaps over the top.

Turn the samosas out of the ramekins on to a greased baking sheet. Brush with melted butter and top with flaked almonds. Bake in a preheated oven at 190°C (375°F) mark 5 for about 20 minutes or until the pastry and almonds are golden brown.

Meanwhile, make the citrus sauce. Peel and segment the orange, discarding all pith and pips; chop the flesh. Put the chopped orange, fruit juices and spices in a saucepan and bring to the boil. Remove from the heat and liquidize, using a blender.

Gradually stir in sugar to taste, then return to the heat and bring to a simmer. Add the Cointreau if using. Blend the arrowroot with a little water, then add to the sauce. Cook, stirring, until slightly thickened.

Place the samosas on warmed serving plates and pour the sauce around. Sprinkle the sauce with orange and lemon rind, and pistachio nuts. Garnish with coriander leaves. Serve with Pumkin and Pineapple Chutney (page 117); Chick Pea Salad in Coconut Dressing (page 108); and potato and Cauliflower Bhaji (page 120).

Nicholas Pound

Right: *Vegetable, Fruit and Nut Samosas*

Pecan and Chestnut Casserole

in Red Wine

125 g (4 oz) dried chestnuts
125 g (4 oz) carrots
125 g (4 oz) baby onions
45 ml (3 tbsp) olive oil
30 ml (2 tbsp) chopped mixed herbs (sage, rosemary and thyme)
300 ml (½ pint) red wine
50 g (2 oz) buckwheat
175 g (6 oz) button mushroms
50 g (2 oz) gram flour
15 ml (1 tbsp) soy sauce
175 g (6 oz) Brussel sprouts
125 g (4 oz) pecan nuts

Put the dried chestnuts in a saucepan with 1.2 litres (2 pints) of water and bring to the boil. Cover and simmer for 25-30 minutes. Drain, reserving the liquid.

Meanwhile cut the carrots into pieces, similar in size to the onions. Heat 30 ml (2 tbsp) oil in a flameproof casserole, add the whole baby onions and fry, stirring for about 3 minutes. Add the carrots and fry the onions and carrots together over a low heat for a few minutes, turning them in the oil.

Add the chestnuts and reserved liquid together with the herbs and a third of the red wine. Cover and cook in a preheated oven at 190°C (375°F) mark 5 for 25 minutes.

Heat 15 ml (1 tbsp) oil in a frying pan and stir-fry the buckwheat for 3 minutes. Add the mushrooms and fry, stirring, for 2 minutes.

Bring the remaining red wine to the boil in a small pan and sprinkle in the gram flour. Simmer, stirring, for 3-5 minutes until the wine begins to thicken, then add the soy sauce.

Add the thickened red wine to the casserole with the buckwheat, mushrooms, Brussel sprouts and pecan nuts. Return to the oven for a further 20 minutes. Sprinkle with pepper to serve.

Janet Dimmer

Cornucopia of Wild Mushrooms and Chestnuts

in Madeira

Pastry:
225 g (8 oz) plain flour
pinch of salt
50 g (2 oz) sunflower spread
50 g (2 oz) butter

Filling:
25 g (1 oz) butter
3 cloves garlic, finely chopped
225 g (8 oz) shallots, finely chopped
350 g (12 oz) mushrooms, chopped
50 g (2 oz) stoned prunes, chopped
25 g (1 oz) dried chestnuts, reconstituted (see note) and chopped
few sage leaves, chopped
¼ bottle Madeira

To Glaze:
1 egg yolk, mixed with a little water

Left: *Pecan and Chestnut Casserole in Red Wine*

Cook's Note

I have found that the best way to reconstitute dried chestnuts is to cover them with water and cook gently in a low oven for about 1 hour.

To make the pastry, sift the flour and salt into a bowl and rub in the fat until the mixture resembles breadcrumbs. Bind with a little water. Wrap the pastry in cling film and leave to rest in the refrigerator.

For the filling, heat the butter in a pan, add the garlic and shallots and cook gently until softened. Add the mushrooms to the pan and cook for 5 minutes. Add the prunes, chestnuts and sage, cook for a few minutes, then add the Madeira. Remove from the heat and allow to stand for an hour if possible.

Roll out the pastry and cut into 1cm (½ inch) strips, then wind around cream horn tins, overlapping the strips. Brush with egg glaze and bake in a preheated oven at 190°C (375°F) mark 5 for 20 minutes. Bring the mushroom filling to a simmer, stirring occasionally, and reduce slightly.

Remove the pastry horns from their moulds and spoon in the mushroom filling. Arrange on individual plates with plenty of the filling spilling out of the horns.

Sarah Beattie

"Oh, that is magnificent."

Ken Livingstone

Leeks with Feta Cheese

and Thyme en Croute

4 large leeks
salt
450 g (1 lb) packet puff pastry
zahtar to taste (see below)
extra-virgin olive oil, for sprinkling
400 g (14 oz) feta cheese, crumbled
beaten egg to glaze

'Burnt' Aubergine and Mint Sauce:
2 medium aubergines
salt
oil for deep-frying
500 ml (16 fl oz) Greek yogurt
juice of 1 lemon
1 clove garlic
mint sprigs, to garnish

To make the 'burnt' aubergine and mint sauce, peel the aubergines and cut the flesh into cubes. Sprinkle with salt and leave to degorge for 15 minutes. Rinse and pat dry with kitchen paper.

Heat the oil in a deep-fryer. When it is very hot, add the aubergine cubes and fry until golden brown. Remove and drain on kitchen paper. Place in a food processor or blender, add the remaining ingredients and work to a smooth sauce. Cool.

Trim the leeks to 10 cm (4 inch) lengths. Place in a pan of boiling salted water, remove from the heat and let stand for 5 minutes. Drain the leeks thoroughly and set aside.

Meanwhile roll out the puff pastry on a lightly floured surface. Cut out four 12 x 7.5 cm (5 x 3 inch) sheets and four slightly larger sheets. Spread a line of zahtar along the middle of each of the smaller pastry sheets, then sprinkle a line of olive oil on top. Cover with a line of feta cheese.

Halve the leeks lengthwise, without cutting right through, then open out and dampen the centres with a sprinkling of water. Place cutside down on the line of feta. Brush the edges of the pastry with beaten egg and position the larger pastry squares on top. Press the edges together to seal, trim and decorate with shapes cut from the pastry trimmings. Brush with egg to glaze. Bake in a preheated oven at 200°C (400°F) mark 6 for 25-30 minutes until golden brown.

Serve immediately, with the 'burnt' aubergine and mint sauce.

Alasdair Friend

"That sauce is a triumph."

Sue MacGregor

• INGREDIENTS •

For this dish, you will need zahtar, a Middle Eastern condiment – of thyme, sesame seeds and lemon juice – available from specialist shops and delicatessens. Make sure you use feta prepared from cow's milk, as it has a superior flavour.

ACCOMPANIMENTS

Wilted Spinach Salad

350 g (12 oz) young spinach leaves, trimmed
few young dandelion leaves or nettle tops (optional)
1 small head red chicory, thinly sliced
40 g (1½ oz) hazelnuts, toasted and skinned
25 ml (5 tsp) light olive or grapeseed oil
15 ml (1 tbsp) hazelnut oil
few juniper berries (optional)
pinch of black pepper
175 g (6 oz) oyster mushrooms
5-7.5 ml (1 tsp) Dijon mustard (preferably hazelnut-flavoured)
pinch of sea salt
15 ml (1 tbsp) medium-sweet Madeira (preferably Bual)
10 ml (2 tsp) balsamic or wine vinegar

Warm a large serving or mixing bowl by rinsing in hot water, then dry thoroughly. Place the salad leaves, sliced chicory or radishes and toasted nuts in the bowl. Warm 15 ml (1 tsp) light olive or grapeseed oil with the hazelnut oil and infuse with the juniper berries if using. Discard the berries, mix the oil with the black pepper and add to the salad leaves. Toss lightly.

Roughly slice the mushrooms and place in a non-stick pan with 10 ml (2 tsp) light olive or grapeseed oil, the mustard and salt. Stir thoroughly, over a medium heat, then cook until the juices begin to run. Remove the lid, increase the heat and drive off the liquid, stirring constantly. Add the Madeira and reduce once more until dry. Add the vinegar, stir around, then immediately pour the mushroom mixture over the leaves and nuts. Toss thoroughly and serve warm.

Silvija Davidson

Mixed Leaf and Walnut Salad

200 g (7 oz) mixed salad leaves, eg radicchio, endive, sorrel, lollo rosso, frisée, oakleaf, lamb's lettuce, watercress
50 g (2 oz) shelled walnuts

Dressing:
10 ml (2 tsp) sherry vinegar
10 ml (2 tsp) balsamic vinegar
45 ml (3 tbsp) walnut oil
10 ml (2 tsp) olive oil
2.5 ml (½ tsp) Dijon mustard
½ clove garlic, crushed
salt and freshly ground pepper

Put the salad leaves in a bowl. Briefly immerse the walnuts in boiling water to remove the skins, then drain and pat dry. Break into small pieces and add to the salad leaves.

Put the vinegar, oil, mustard, garlic, salt and pepper in a screw-topped jar and shake vigorously to combine.

Pour the dressing over the salad and toss to mix. Divide between individual plates to serve.

Amita Baldock

Right: *Mixed Leaf and Walnut Salad*

Papillote of Roast Vegetables

1 medium fennel bulb
1 stick celery
1 courgette
4 thick asparagus spears
4 baby carrots, with leaves
4 baby waxy potatoes (preferably pink fir apple variety)
4 button onions
4 large dried morels, pre-soaked and drained
60 ml (4 tbsp) clarified butter
15 ml (1 tbsp) sugar
15 ml (1 tbsp) salt
4 tarragon sprigs
4 thyme sprigs
4 cloves garlic
20 black peppercorns

"Very good idea"

Antonio Carluccio

Cut the fennel bulb into quarters. Cut the celery into four 7.5cm (3 inch) strips. Cut the courgette into four 7.5cm (3 inch) lengths. Trim the asparagus spears to 7.5cm (3 inch) lengths. Place all the vegetables in a bowl. Melt the clarified butter and stir in the sugar and salt. Pour over the vegetables and turn to coat them evenly.

Take four A4 sheets of greaseproof paper, fold each one in half, then open again. Place each portion of vegetables at one side of the fold. Add the herbs, garlic and 5 peppercorns per parcel. Fold the greaseproof paper over the vegetables. To make the papillotes, refer to the diagram below. Place on a baking sheet and cook in a preheated oven at 200°C (400°F) mark 6 for 20 minutes. Serve on warmed plates. Leave the papillotes for your guests to open themselves.

Jo Eitel

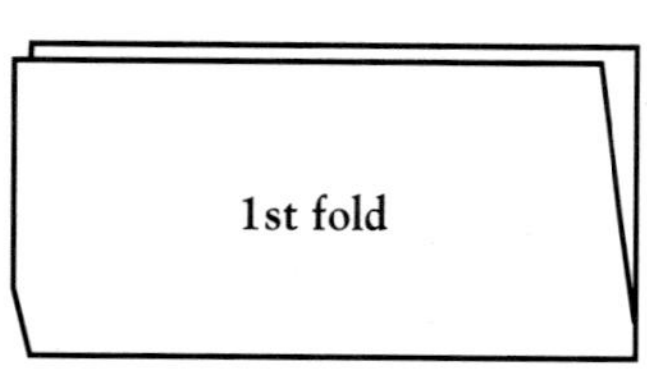

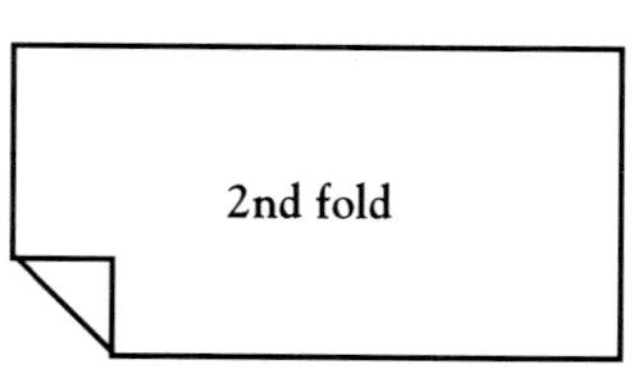

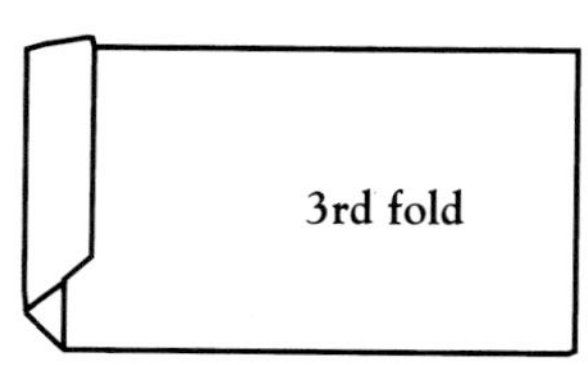

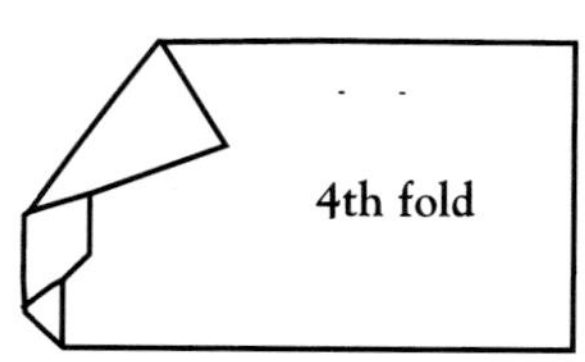

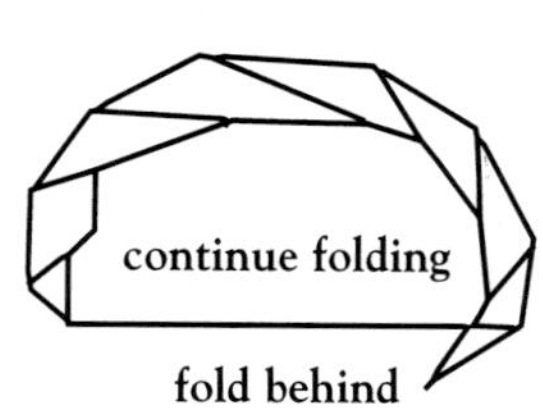

Parsley Profiteroles

with Horseradish Cream

50 g (2 oz) butter
150 ml (¼ pint) water
65 g (2½ oz) plain flour
2 eggs, beaten
15 ml (1 tbsp) finely chopped parsley
pinch of salt

Horseradish Cream:
300 ml (½ pint) soured cream (see note)
30 ml (2 tbsp) grated fresh horseradish
salt and freshly ground black pepper

Heat the butter and water in a saucepan until the butter has melted. Bring to the boil, remove from the heat and beat in the flour to form a smooth paste. Cool slightly, then gradually add the eggs, beating all the time. Add the chopped parsley and salt.

Spoon 16 balls of dough on to a greased baking sheet. Bake in a preheated oven at 220°C (425°F) mark 7 for 20 minutes until golden brown and crisp. Split and pop back in the oven for a few minutes to cook the inside dough if necessary.

For the horseradish cream, mix the soured cream with the grated horseradish and seasoning to taste. Use to fill the profiteroles.

Linda Yewdall

• Cook's Note •

Sour double cream by adding a drop of lime juice. I always use limes in preference to lemons because a lime is a lemon with a sunny disposition!

Stir-fried Broccoli

with Ginger

450 g (1 lb) broccoli
salt
30 ml (2 tbsp) corn oil
1 clove garlic, thinly sliced
2.5 cm (1 inch) piece fresh root ginger, finely shredded
2.5 ml (½ tsp) sesame oil

Separate the broccoli spears into florets and cut the base of the stems diagonally to give a neat appearance. Blanch in a saucepan of boiling salted water for 30 seconds. Drain and refresh in cold water; drain thoroughly.

Heat the oil in a wok or frying pan, add the garlic and ginger and stir-fry for 30 seconds. Add the broccoli and stir-fry for 2 minutes.

Sprinkle over the sesame oil and stir-fry for 30 seconds only. Serve immediately.

Betsy Anderson

"*Absolutely fabulous*"

Valentina Harris

Tagliatelle of Courgette and Mangetout

125 g (4 oz) small courgettes
125 g (4 oz) mangetouts
7.5 ml (½ tbsp) sesame oil

Cut the courgettes into 3 mm (⅛ inch) slices, then into thin strips. Trim the mangetouts and cut lengthwise into thin strips. Mix the courgettes and mangetouts together and microwave for 2 minutes, then drain. When ready to serve, heat the sesame oil in a pan, add the vegetables and mix gently to reheat.

Vanessa Binns

Cook's Tip

If you do not have a microwave oven, cook the courgettes and mangetout separately in boiling salted water, allowing 1 minute for the courgettes, 1½ minutes for the mangetout. Drain well before tossing in the sesame oil.

Courgette Fritters

225 g (8 oz) courgettes
60 ml (4 tbsp) plain flour
salt and freshly ground pepper
sunflower oil, for shallow-frying

Cut the courgettes into diagonal 5 mm (¼ inch) slices. Mix the flour with enough water to form a creamy batter. Season with salt and pepper. Pour oil into a large frying pan to a depth of 1cm (½ inch) and place over moderate heat.

When the oil is hot, dip the courgettes into the batter to coat; then fry, a few at a time, until golden brown, turning as necessary. Drain on kitchen paper, sprinkle with salt and keep warm in the oven while cooking the remainder. Serve as soon as possible.

Jennifer Twydell

Stir-fried Mangetouts

with Garlic

225 g (8 oz) mangetouts
15 ml (1 tbsp) olive oil
2 cloves garlic, finely chopped

Top and tail the mangetouts. Heat the olive oil in a wok or deep frying pan and stir-fry the garlic for 2 minutes. Add the mangetouts together with 30 ml (2 tbsp) water and stir-fry for 2 minutes. Serve immediately.

Janet Dimmer

Chick Pea Salad

in Coconut Dressing

450 g (1 lb) cooked chick peas

Dressing:
250 ml (8 fl oz) creamed coconut
150 ml (5 fl oz) natural yogurt
15 ml (1 tbsp) finely chopped coriander leaves
10 ml (2 tsp) clear honey
30 ml (2 tbsp) desiccated coconut
5 ml (1 tsp) mustard
pinch of salt
pinch of cayenne pepper

To Garnish:
coriander sprigs

Place the chick peas in a serving bowl. Combine the ingredients for the dressing in a jug. Stir well, then pour over the chick peas and toss well. Chill before serving, garnished with coriander sprigs.

Nicholas Pound

Seasonal Salad Leaves and Herbs

with Balsamic Dressing

selection of salad leaves, eg lamb's lettuce, lollo rosso, oakleaf lettuce and watercress
selection of salad herbs, eg chervil, dill, sweet cicely, bronze fennel

Dressing:
15 ml (1 tbsp) balsamic vinegar
2.5 ml (½ tsp) Dijon mustard
coarse sea salt
freshly ground pepper
75 ml (5 tbsp) extra-virgin olive oil (approximately)

Combine all the salad leaves in a bowl. Add the herbs, which should be roughly torn if large.

To make the dressing, mix the vinegar with the mustard and seasoning in a small bowl. Whisk in enough olive oil to give a thick emulsion.

Pour the dressing over the salad and toss lightly to serve.

Sue Lawrence

Filo Pastry Baskets

of Seasonal Vegetables

75 g (3 oz) butter, melted
6 sheets filo pastry
2 carrots
2 courgettes
4 broccoli florets
4 cauliflower florets
10 ml (2 tsp) finely chopped parsley

Cook's Note

Depending on the size of the filo pastry sheets, you may only be able to cut 3 complete squares. In this case, assemble the fourth from the trimmings.

Cook's Note

Either use canned creamed coconut, or a block of creamed coconut and follow packet directions for use.

Behind the Scenes...

"I always wear ties with edible motifs. Throughout the series my ties have featured snails, ducks, chickens, rabbits and assorted fish. Snails is my favourite – to look at not to eat – and made its debut in honour of Albert Roux. There is a sad shortage of ties decorated with fruit and vegetables, but I keep looking."

...Loyd

Right: *Filo Pastry Baskets of Seasonal Vegetables*

Use one third of the butter to prepare the filo baskets. Grease 4 patty tins. Lay a sheet of filo on the work surface, brush with melted butter and cover with a second layer of pastry. Brush with melted butter and cover with a third layer. Using a sharp knife, cut out four 12 cm (5 inch) squares (see note). Place each triple layer of squares in a patty tin, pressing the pastry into the base of the tin and allowing the edges to spread out like a handkerchief. Use the trimming to make handles, if you wish; place these on a baking tray.

Bake in a preheated oven at 200°C (400°F) mark 6 for 8-10 minutes until the pastry is golden brown. Allow to cool in the tins, then remove and set aside.

To prepare the carrots and courgettes, cut into 4 cm (1½ inch) lengths and shape into batons. Place in a steaming basket with the broccoli and cauliflower. Cook until the vegetables are just tender.

In a bowl, stir together the remaining 50 g (2 oz) butter and chopped parsley. Add the hot vegetables and toss gently to coat in the butter. Place each pastry basket on a small plate and divide the vegetables between them. Add a pastry handle to each basket, if using, and serve at once.

Jane O'Sullivan

Spinach with Nutmeg

450 g (1 lb) young spinach leaves
7.5 ml (½ tbsp) hazelnut oil
7.5 ml (½ tbsp) olive oil
15 g (½ oz) shallot, finely chopped
2 cloves garlic, crushed
freshly grated nutmeg
coarse sea salt
freshly ground pepper

Roughly tear the spinach leaves. Heat the hazelnut and olive oils in a pan, add the shallot and garlic and sweat for about 2 minutes. Add the torn spinach leaves, with just the water clinging to their leaves after washing. Sauté briefly for about 2 minutes, then season liberally with nutmeg, salt and pepper. Serve immediately.

Sue Lawrence

Sauté of Spinach and Watercress

250 g (9 oz) washed spinach
150 g (5 oz) washed watercress, longer stalks removed
30 ml (2 tbsp) quality extra-virgin olive oil
salt and freshly ground black pepper

Tear the leaves of the spinach and mix with the watercress. Heat the oil in a frying pan and when it is really hot, add the spinach and watercress mixture. Sauté for about 30 seconds only. Season with salt and pepper to taste and serve immediately.

Helen Pothecary

Filo Parcels of Spinach

with Lemon, Nutmeg and Garlic

700 g (1½ lb) fresh spinach, washed and stalks removed
75 g (3 oz) unsalted butter
1 clove garlic, crushed
twelve 10 cm (4 inch) squares of filo pastry
50 g (2 oz) butter, melted
salt and freshly ground black pepper
5 ml (1 tsp) freshly grated nutmeg
7.5 ml (1½ tsp) lemon juice

Pat the spinach dry with absorbent kitchen paper. Melt the unsalted butter in a large deep pan with the garlic over a low heat, then add the spinach. Cover and cook over a moderate heat, stirring occasionally, for about 3-4 minutes until the spinach softens and wilts.

Brush 3 squares of filo pastry with melted butter and pile on top of each other, at an angle, to form a 'star' shape. Season the spinach with salt, pepper and nutmeg. Add the lemon juice. Place a heaped spoonful of spinach in the centre of the pastry star. Bring the corners up over the filling and scrunch together to form a parcel. Repeat to make another three parcels. Place on a lightly greased baking tray. Cover and refrigerate for 1 hour.

Bake the filo parcels in a preheated oven at 200°C (400°F) mark 6 for 10-15 minutes, until golden brown and crisp. Serve at once.

Vera Bloor

Butter-cooked Lettuce

2 Little Gem or small Cos lettuce
salt and freshly ground black pepper
sugar, to taste
15 ml (1 tbsp) butter

Trim each lettuce, slice in half lengthwise and season with salt, pepper and sugar to taste. Heat the butter in a frying pan, add the lettuce and fry very gently, turning occasionally for about 15-20 minutes until each side is browned. Serve immediately.

Orlando Murrin

Cook's Note

Cooked lettuce has a delicate flavour all of its own – quite unlike any other leaf vegetable.

Aubergine Purée

with Pine Nuts

450 g (1 lb) aubergines
40 g (1½ oz) butter, softened
75 g (3 oz) full-fat cream cheese with garlic
1.25 ml (¼ tsp) cayenne pepper
salt
40 g (1½ oz) pine nuts
coriander leaves, to garnish

Place the whole unpeeled aubergines under a preheated high grill for approximately 15-20 minutes, turning continuously until they are black all over and the skin has blistered. Holding the hot aubergines in a cloth, break them open and scrape the flesh out into a food processor or blender, using a metal spoon.

Add the butter and soft cheese and work to a smooth purée. Season to taste with cayenne pepper and salt. Spoon the mixture into a warm serving bowl.

Heat a small dry frying pan and add the pine nuts. Toss for 1-2 minutes or until toasted dark brown.

Scatter the nuts over the aubergine purée. Cover the dish with foil and keep warm in a low oven until ready to serve. Garnish with a sprinkling of cayenne pepper and coriander leaves.

Jane O'Sullivan

Leeks with Warm Vinaigrette

4 medium leeks

Vinaigrette:
5 ml (1 tsp) Dijon mustard
15 ml (1 tbsp) blueberry vinegar
coarse sea salt
freshly ground pepper
45-75 ml (3-5 tbsp) olive oil

Cut the leeks diagonally into slices and steam over boiling water for 2 minutes, until cooked but still crunchy. Drain.

For the vinaigrette, mix together the mustard, vinegar and seasoning to taste. Whisk in enough olive oil to give a thick emulsion.

Toss the leeks in the vinaigrette and serve immediately.

Sue Lawrence

Buttered Leeks

with Tarragon

450 g (1 lb) young leeks
50-75 g (2-3 oz) butter
1 large bunch of tarragon
salt and freshly ground black pepper

Trim the leeks and cut into 7.5 cm (3 inch) lengths. Cut each piece lengthways into 4 slices and wash thoroughly. Drain and pat dry with kitchen paper. Tie half of the tarragon into a bunch with cotton string.

Melt the butter in a saucepan. Add the leeks and tarragon bunch to the pan and stir well. Cover and cook over a low heat, shaking the pan occasionally, for 10 minutes or until the leeks are tender but still retain their colour. Meanwhile, strip the remaining tarragon leaves from their stalks and chop finely.

Just before serving, discard the bunch of tarragon. Add the chopped tarragon to the leeks, stir and season with salt and pepper to taste. Serve immediately.

Patti Hall

Behind the Scenes...

"Practice and attention to detail makes for winning performances – a fact perhaps not fully appreciated by the long suffering families of our contestants who are invariably the guinea pigs for MasterChef menus. Most of them never want to taste their beloved's most accomplished dishes ever again."

...Loyd

Braised Red Cabbage

10 ml (2 tsp) olive oil
15 g (½ oz) butter
50 g (2 oz) unsmoked bacon, derinded and chopped
1 onion, chopped
2 cloves garlic, crushed
450 g (1 lb) red cabbage, sliced
1 cooking apple
300 ml (½ pint) mixed red wine and stock
pinch of cloves
freshly grated nutmeg
1.25 ml (¼ tsp) salt
freshly ground pepper

Heat the oil and butter in a large pan and sauté the bacon, onion and garlic until softened. Add the red cabbage and cook, stirring, for 10 minutes.

Peel, core and chop the apple. Add to the cabbage with the remaining ingredients and bring to the boil.

Transfer to an ovenproof dish, cover and cook in a preheated oven at 160°C (325°F) mark 3 for 2-3 hours until tender.

Sue Lawrence

Baby Vegetables en Papillote

12 baby carrots
8 cauliflower florets
12 baby corn cobs
12 mangetouts
8 broccoli florets
salt and freshly ground black pepper
5 bouquet garnis, tied with string

Herb Butter:
125 g (4 oz) butter, softened
10-15 ml (2-3 tsp) herbs
5-10 ml (1-2 tsp) lemon juice

First make the herb butter. Put the butter, herbs and lemon juice in a bowl and mix well. Season with salt and pepper to taste. Set aside.

Bring a large pan of water to the boil. Add the carrots and cauliflower and parboil for about 3 minutes, then remove with a slotted spoon.

Place a bamboo steamer over the pan of boiling water and place all of the vegetables in the steamer, together with one of the herb bouquets. Cover and steam the vegetables for 6 minutes. Remove the steamer from the heat.

Distribute the vegetables evenly between 4 buttered sheets of greaseproof paper, placing them in the centre of the paper. Sprinkle with a little salt and top each portion with a spoonful of the herb butter. Bring the two ends of the paper together, then roll down leaving enough space for air to circulate. Twist the two open ends and secure with wooden clothes pegs. Place in a microwave oven and cook on high for 30 seconds.

Serve the vegetables in their paper packets. Garnish each serving with a bouquet of herbs.

Betsy Anderson

Cook's Note

For the papillotes you will need 4 sheets of greaseproof paper and ideally 8 wooden clothes pegs, or heat-resistant plastic clips.

Cook's Tip

Reheating the vegetables by microwave ensures that they retain their bright colours. Alternatively you could return to the steamer to heat through.

Right: *Baby Vegetables en Papillote*

Parsnips with Ricotta and Soured Cream

825 g (1¾ lb) parsnips
3 spring onions, chopped
75 g (3 oz) ricotta cheese
150 ml (¼ pint) soured cream
25 g (1 oz) gruyère cheese, grated
15 ml (1 tbsp) fresh white breadcrumbs
salt and freshly ground pepper
freshly grated nutmeg

Cut the parsnips into 5 mm (¼ inch) slices and place in a saucepan. Add salted water to cover, bring to the boil and simmer for 2-3 minutes; drain thoroughly.

Mix the spring onions with the ricotta until evenly blended. Layer the parsnips, ricotta mixture and soured cream in a buttered ovenproof dish, seasoning each layer liberally with salt and pepper and finishing with a layer of soured cream. Scatter the gruyère, breadcrumbs and nutmeg over the top. Cover and cook in a preheated oven at 180°C (350°F) mark 4 for 45-50 minutes, removing the lid for the last 10 minutes to brown the tops.

Lynda Hinton

"There's a nice sharp bite to that."

Angela Rippon

Parsnip Timbales

with Asparagus and Broad Beans

900 g (2 lb) young parsnips
salt and freshly ground black pepper
1 clove garlic, finely chopped
5 ml (1 tsp) finely chopped thyme leaves
120 ml (4 fl oz) double cream
3 eggs, size 3, lightly beaten
1 red pepper
350 g (12 oz) shelled fresh or frozen broad beans
1 bunch of pencil-thin young asparagus spears
5 ml (1 tsp) butter
3 shallots, very finely chopped
250 ml (8 fl oz) crème fraîche

Butter 4 dariole moulds. Peel and quarter the parsnips, then remove the cores. Add to a pan of cold salted water and bring to the boil. Cook until tender, about 15 minutes; drain well.

Transfer the cooked parsnips to a food processor or blender and work to a purée. Add seasoning, garlic, thyme and the cream. Process briefly until evenly mixed. Transfer the mixture to a bowl and stir in the eggs.

Halve the pepper, discarding the core and seeds. Cook under a preheated hot grill until the skin is blackened. Place in a dish, cover tightly and leave until cool enough to handle, then peel away the skin. Cut one half into 8 strips, cut the other half into 16-20 small diamond-shaped pieces.

Place 2 red pepper strips on opposite sides of each dariole mould, then fill with the parsnip mixture. Cover each one with a circle of buttered greaseproof paper. Place the moulds in a roasting tin containing enough cold water to come halfway up the sides. Cook in a preheated oven at 220°C (425°F) mark 7 for 25 minutes until a skewer inserted into the centre comes out clean.

Meanwhile blanch the broad beans in boiling water for 3-4 minutes. Drain, refresh in cold water and drain again. Slip off the skins. Set aside about 24 broad beans for the garnish; keep warm. Steam the asparagus for about 8-10 minutes.

Meanwhile, to make the sauce, melt the butter in a pan and sauté the shallots until soft. Add the rest of the broad beans and sauté for 2 minutes. Stir in the crème fraîche and bring to the boil. Simmer for a few seconds. Pass through a fine sieve into a bowl; thin with a little water if necessary.

Unmould a parsnip timbale onto each warmed plate and arrange red pepper diamonds on the top. Surround with the sauce. Arrange the asparagus spears on the plates, interspersed with the reserved broad beans. Serve immediately.

Ross Burden

Tagliatelle of Carrots

225 g (8 oz) carrots
30 ml (2 tbsp) sunflower oil
25 g (1 oz) white mustard seeds
salt

Peel the carrots and, using a paring knife or potato peeler, pare the carrots into long thin ribbons to resemble tagliatelle.

Heat the oil in a small pan until hot, but not smoking. Add the mustard seeds and shake the pan for about 10 seconds only, until the seeds begin to pop. Immediately remove the pan from the heat, cover and wait until the seeds stop popping.

Add the carrot tagliatelle to the pan and mix well to coat in the oil. Cover and cook over a medium heat for 2-3 minutes; the carrots should retain some 'bite'. Check the seasoning, adding a little salt, if desired. Serve immediately.

Kerry Church

Celeriac Rösti

1 celeriac
salt and freshly ground black pepper
25 g (1 oz) butter

Peel and quarter the celeriac, then grate coarsely into a bowl. Season with salt and pepper. Divide the mixture into 4 portions. Press each portion into a muffin ring or 7.5 cm (3 inch) plain metal cutter, resting on a fish slice or spatula.

Melt the butter in a frying pan and carefully slide the rings into the pan. Press the celeriac well down in the rings and fry for 3-4 minutes until crisp and golden brown underneath.

Turn the rösti, carefully remove the rings and cook the other side for 3-4 minutes until golden brown and cooked through. Drain on kitchen paper. Serve at once.

Derek Johns

Gratin of Jerusalem Artichokes

500 g (1 lb) Jerusalem artichokes
salt and freshly ground black pepper
15 ml (1 tbsp) unsalted butter
300 ml (½ pint) double cream

Slice the Jerusalem artichokes into 5 mm (¼ inch) rings. Season with salt and pepper. Layer the artichoke slices in a buttered gratin dish. Dot with butter and pour over the cream. Cook in a preheated oven at 180°C (350°F) mark 4 for 15-20 minutes until tender.

Helen Pothecary

Horseradish and Ginger Röstis

2.5 cm (1 inch) piece fresh root ginger, grated
25 g (1 oz) fresh horseradish, grated
2 large potatoes, peeled and grated
salt and freshly ground black pepper
125 g (4 oz) butter, melted

Put the grated ginger in a small saucepan, add water to cover, bring to the boil and simmer for 5 minutes. Drain, refresh in cold water; drain.

Put the grated potato in a clean tea-towel and squeeze out all the moisture. Turn into a large bowl and add the ginger and horseradish, salt and pepper. Carefully mix well with a fork to disperse the flavourings evenly. Stir in 45 ml (3 tbsp) melted butter.

Heat the remaining butter in a pan until foaming. Place a greased 10 cm (4 inch) muffin ring in the pan and fill with a quarter of the potato mixture. Press down well and remove the ring. Repeat to shape a further 3 rostis. Cook on one side for approximately 5 minutes until golden. Turn carefully and cook the other side. Drain on absorbent kitchen paper for a few seconds, then transfer to a wire rack to retain crispness. Reheat the röstis in a hot oven for a few minutes before serving.

Gregory Lewis

Gâteaux of Vegetables

2 carrots, peeled and cut into pieces
salt and freshly ground black pepper
2.5 ml (½ tsp) sugar
25 g (1 oz) unsalted butter, plus a knob
200 g (7 oz) spinach, thoroughly washed and drained
1 clove garlic, crushed
20 ml (4 tsp) olive oil
2 tomatoes, peeled, seeded and chopped
2 courgettes, thinly sliced
1 large parsnip, peeled and sliced
2 basil leaves, shredded

Cook the carrots in a little salted water, with the sugar added, until tender. Drain and chop finely or purée in a food processor with a knob of butter.

Melt 15 g (½ oz) butter in a pan. Remove any coarse stalks from the spinach, then add to the pan with the garlic. Cook over a fairly high heat for a few minutes until the spinach is tender and excess moisture has evaporated. Drain on absorbent kitchen paper.

Heat half the olive oil in a pan, add the chopped tomatoes and cook for a few minutes until soft. Fry the courgettes in the remaining olive oil for about 2 minutes until softened.

Parboil the parsnips in salted water for 2-3 minutes. Drain and refresh in cold water. Dry on absorbent kitchen paper, then grate. Mix with the remaining 15 g (½ oz) butter and cook gently until lightly coloured.

Line 4 loose-based 10 cm (4 inch) moulds with foil and pierce the foil in several places. Adjust the seasoning of the vegetables to taste.

To assemble each gâteau, spoon a portion of spinach into the base of each mould and press down well. Add a layer of carrot and press down. Place the courgette slices around the edge, slightly overlapping them to form a well. Add the chopped basil to the tomato and spoon into the well. Fill the moulds to the top with parsnip, pressing down well. Reheat the gâteaux in a steamer, then turn out before serving.

Gregory Lewis

COOK'S NOTE

These individual gâteaux are cooked in loose-based moulds to allow any excess water to drain away. Alternatively you can use rings and seal the bases with pierced foil. The gâteaux can be reheated in the microwave, but the foil must be removed first.

GLAZED RADISHES

36 small radishes
50 g (2 oz) butter
salt and freshly ground black pepper
5 ml (1 tsp) sugar

Trim the radishes, leaving the root points and a short stalk on each one. Place in a small pan with the butter, salt and pepper, and the sugar. Add enough water to half-cover the radishes and bring to the boil. Lower the heat and simmer for about 10 minutes until the water is reduced and the butter coats the radishes in a shiny glaze. Serve at once.

Brian Tompkins

PUMPKIN AND PINEAPPLE CHUTNEY

1 small onion, chopped
175 g (6 oz) pumpkin, diced
225 g (8 oz) can pineapple chunks in natural juice
5 ml (1 tsp) ground cinnamon
5 ml (1 tsp) ground ginger
10 ml (2 tsp) chopped fresh coriander leaves
250 ml (8 fl oz) wine or cider vinegar
1 vegetable stock cube, crumbled
30 ml (2 tbsp) brown sugar
50 g (2 oz) raisins

To Garnish:
chopped pistachio nuts

Place all the ingredients, except the raisins, in a saucepan. Bring to the boil, cover and simmer for 30 minutes or until the pumpkin is very tender.

Remove from the heat and work briefly, using a blender or food processor; the chutney should retain some chunky pieces. Stir in the raisins.

With a slotted spoon, ladle the chutney into a serving bowl, then chill until needed. Serve sprinkled with chopped pistachios.

Nicholas Pound

Left: *Gâteaux of Vegetables*

FRENCH POTATO CAKE

30 ml (2 tbsp) butter or duck fat
600 g (1¼ lb) potatoes, peeled and thinly sliced
2.5 ml (½ tsp) salt
freshly ground pepper
15 g (½ oz) butter, plus extra for greasing
2 garlic cloves, finely chopped
30 ml (2 tbsp) finely chopped parsley

Heat the fat in a heavy-based frying pan and fry the potatoes, partially covered, until lightly browned, about 25 minutes. Season with salt and pepper.

Pack the potatoes into a buttered shallow tart tin or individual flan tins, pressing down firmly. Bake in a preheated oven at 200°C (400°F) mark 6 for about 20 minutes, or until brown and slightly puffy.

Drizzle butter around the edge of the tin, loosen the potato cake and carefully turn out. Cut into wedges and sprinkle with the garlic and parsley to serve.

Orlando Murrin

SHREDDED POTATO PANCAKES

450 g (1 lb) potatoes, peeled
60 g (2½ oz) butter, softened
salt and freshly ground black pepper

Shred the potatoes, then squeeze to remove excess liquid and starch. Mix with half of the softened butter. Season with salt and pepper.

Heat the remaining butter in a large frying pan, divide the potato mixture into 4 portions and form into pancakes. Fry in the hot butter for about 5 minutes on each side until golden brown.

Vanessa Binns

PAN-FRIED ROSEMARY POTATOES

4 large potatoes
knob of unsalted butter
15 ml (1 tbsp) olive oil
4 rosemary sprigs

Peel the potatoes, trim the edges square, then cut into small cubes and place in cold water. Just before cooking, drain and pat dry with kitchen paper.

Heat the butter and oil in a large heavy-based pan. Add the potato cubes with the rosemary and cook, tossing frequently, until the potatoes are crisp and brown on the outside and cooked through. Drain on absorbent kitchen paper. Serve immediately.

Timothy Stokes

FONDANT POTATOES

WITH SESAME SEEDS

450 g (1 lb) small new potatoes
65 g (2½ oz) unsalted butter
15 ml (1 tbsp) sesame seeds
salt

Scrape the potatoes, rinse in cold water and dry them in a cloth.

Melt two thirds of the butter in a sauté pan. Add the potatoes and shake the pan to coat the potatoes with butter. Cover the pan and cook over a moderate heat for 20-30 minutes, shaking the pan now and then to prevent the potatoes from sticking.

When cooked, remove the lid and increase the heat to drive off any surplus moisture and give the potatoes a crisp finish. Add the remaining butter and, when melted, add the sesame seeds. Shake the pan until the potatoes are evenly coated with sesame seeds. Serve immediately.

Jane O'Sullivan

Right: *French Potato Cake* (top); *Fondant Potatoes with Sesame Seeds* (centre); *Shredded Potato Pancakes* (below)

Potato and Cauliflower Bhaji

450 g (1 lb) potatoes
25 g (1 oz) butter or margarine
1 large onion, sliced into rings
2 cloves garlic, chopped
15 ml (1 tbsp) minced fresh chilli pepper
10 ml (2 tsp) ground cumin
10 ml (2 tsp) ground coriander
10 ml (2 tsp) garam masala
1 small cauliflower, divided into florets
salt and freshly ground black pepper
30 ml (2 tbsp) olive oil

Peel the potatoes, then grate them into a bowl of cold water. Melt the butter or margarine in a non-stick frying pan and gently fry the onion and garlic until softened. Add the chilli, and 5 ml (1 tsp) each of cumin, coriander and garam masala. Heat through, stirring, for 1 minute, then remove from the heat.

Drain the grated potato and squeeze out excess liquid using your hands. Add to the frying pan and stir to coat in the spices. Return to a low heat.

Slice the cauliflower florets lengthwise; set aside 12 flat floret shapes. Roughly chop the rest of the cauliflower slices and add them to the potato mixture. Stir well, then flatten the mixture, using the back of a wooden spoon, to form an omelette shape. Season well.

Cook the bhaji for 5-10 minutes on each side until golden brown; keep pressing it down with the back of the spoon so that it cooks right through.

In another pan, fry the remaining spices in the olive oil for about 1 minute, then add the reserved cauliflower floret shapes and cook until golden brown.

Either slice the bhaji into quarters in the pan or transfer to a baking sheet and cut out 8 rounds, using a plain pastry cutter. Arrange the fried cauliflower florets on top of the bhaji to serve.

Nicholas Pound

Potato and Wild Mushroom Cakes

250 g (9 oz) potatoes, peeled
7 g (¼ oz) dried mushrooms
450 g (1 lb) cultivated mushrooms
30 ml (2 tbsp) butter
30 ml (2 tbsp) oil
185 ml (6 fl oz) double cream
1 clove garlic, chopped
salt and freshly ground black pepper
butter, for greasing

Cut the potatoes into 3 mm (⅛ inch) slices and immerse in a bowl of cold water. Soak the dried mushrooms in sufficient hot water to cover for 20 minutes. Drain. Cut the cultivated mushrooms into 3 mm (⅛ inch) slices.

Heat the butter and oil in a pan and sauté the cultivated mushrooms to soften. Add the soaked mushrooms and sauté for 1 minute, then add the cream and garlic and reduce until most of the liquid has evaporated. Season with salt and pepper to taste.

Drain the potatoes and dry well. Melt a knob of butter in the base of each of 4 ramekins. Arrange half of the potatoes in the ramekins in overlapping spirals. Cover with a layer of mushrooms, then top with the remaining potatoes. Dot with butter and bake in a preheated oven at 200°C (400°F) mark 6 for 25-30 minutes. Unmould to serve.

Martha Spencer

Garlic Potato Streamers

4 large Desirée potatoes, peeled
125 g (4 oz) unsalted butter
4 cloves garlic, crushed
salt and freshly ground black pepper
freshly grated Parmesan cheese, for sprinkling

Cut the potatoes crosswise into 2.5 cm (1 inch) thick slices. Using a potato peeler, carefully peel around the potato slices to form long ribbons or 'streamers'. Immerse in a bowl of iced water and leave to soak for 1 hour.

Meanwhile melt the butter in a pan, add the garlic and soften gently to flavour the butter. Remove the potato streamers from the water and pat dry on kitchen paper.

Dip the potato streamers in the garlic butter and place on a baking sheet. Season with salt and pepper and sprinkle with a little Parmesan. Roast in a preheated oven at 200°C (400°F) mark 6, for about 12-15 minutes until cooked and golden. Serve immediately.

Brian Tompkins

Lemony Potatoes

450 g (1 lb) small new potatoes, preferably Jersey Royals
1 lemon
30 ml (2 tbsp) soft white breadcrumbs
freshly ground black pepper
coarse sea salt
25 g (1 oz) unsalted butter

Scrape or scrub the potatoes and parboil until just tender. Drain and place in an ovenproof dish. Grate the lemon rind and mix into the breadcrumbs with plenty of freshly ground pepper and a little salt. Squeeze the lemon and sprinkle the juice over the potatoes. Scatter the breadcrumb mixture over the top and dot with small pieces of butter. Bake in a preheated oven at 200°C (400°F) mark 6 for 10-15 minutes until the potatoes are tender.

Sarah Beattie

Puy Lentils

175 g (6 oz) puy lentils
1 onion, chopped
10 ml (2 tsp) dried herbs de Provence
salt and freshly ground black pepper

Put the lentils in a saucepan, add cold water to cover and bring to the boil. Boil rapidly for 5 minutes, then drain and refresh in cold water; drain again.

Put the lentils, onion, herbs and salt and pepper into a large saucepan. Cover with cold water and bring to the boil. Cook until the lentils are tender but not mushy and the water is absorbed – add more water during cooking if necessary.

Amanda Dawson

Cook's Note

The lentils may take anything from 25-40 minutes to cook depending on their type and age, but once cooked they can be kept warm over a low heat or reheated.

DESSERTS

GREEN FIGS EN PAPILLOTE

WITH CHARTREUSE

8 figs
1 large banana
20 ml (4 tsp) sugar
20 ml (4 tsp) unsalted butter
20 ml (4 tsp) green Chartreuse liqueur
melted butter, for brushing

Cut the tips off the figs, then make a cross-cut through the top of each one. Slice the banana diagonally. Cut four 30 cm (12 inches) circles of non-stick baking parchment.

Arrange the banana slices on one half of each circle and sit the figs on top. Sprinkle with the sugar, dot with butter and drizzle over the liqueur. Brush the other half of the paper circles with water to moisten. Brush the edges of the circles with melted butter, then bring the moistened halves over the filling and press the edges together.

To seal each parcel, starting at one end of the semi-circle, fold the edges over to form a series of overlapping tucks. To ensure the pleats do not unroll during cooking, insert a strip of foil into each pleat. Bake in a preheated oven at 220°C (425°F) mark 7 for 6 minutes.

Serve immediately, accompanied by whipped cream flavoured with a little Chartreuse if desired.

Ross Burden

PASSION FRUIT SOUFFLÉ

2 egg yolks
150 g (5 oz) caster sugar
4 egg whites
finely grated rind of ½ lemon

Sauce:
12 passion fruit
65 g (2½ oz) caster sugar
juice of ½ lemon
juice of 1 orange

To Finish:
icing sugar, for dusting

First make the sauce. Cut the passion fruit in half and scoop out the pulp and seeds. Strain and reserve 30 ml (2 tbsp) juice. Put the rest of the pulp and seeds in a pan with the sugar, lemon and orange juices and 5 ml (1 tsp) water. Bring to the boil and simmer for 2 minutes. Strain through a sieve and set aside.

Place a roasting tin half-filled with hot water in a preheated oven at 220°C (425°F) mark 7 to heat. Grease a 12 cm (5 inch) soufflé dish with melted butter and sprinkle lightly with caster sugar.

In a bowl, beat the egg yolks with half of the sugar until pale and fluffy. In another bowl, whisk the egg whites with half of the remaining sugar until they start to thicken. Add the rest of the sugar and whisk to a soft peak consistency.

Mix 30 ml (2 tbsp) of the passion fruit syrup (not the reserved juice) with the grated lemon rind. Stir into the egg yolk mixture. Fold in one third of the whisked egg whites; lightly fold in the remainder.

Pour the mixture into the prepared soufflé dish and place in the roasting tin. Bake for 10-15 minutes until risen and brown.

To serve, add the reserved passion fruit juice to the passion fruit syrup. Heat gently to warm through. When the soufflé is ready, dust with icing sugar and serve immediately, with the warm passion fruit sauce.

Timothy Stokes

"Very good! Absolutely exquisite taste. This is my favourite kind of pudding."

Rose Grey

Right: *Passion Fruit Soufflé*

Bread and Butter Pudding

with Rum and Prunes

6 slices buttered bread
butter, for spreading
350 ml (12 fl oz) single cream
60 ml (4 tbsp) dark rum
few drops of vanilla essence
6 egg yolks
50 g (2 oz) caster sugar
50 g (2 oz) no-soak prunes, stoned and diced

Raspberry Coulis:
175 g (6 oz) raspberries
10 ml (2 tsp) icing sugar
10 ml (2 tsp) lemon juice
10 ml (2 tsp) orange juice

Rum Sabayon:
6 egg yolks
50 g (2 oz) caster sugar
60 ml (4 tbsp) rum
120 ml (4 fl oz) whipping cream, lightly whipped

Butter the bread, discard the crusts, then cut into 2.5 cm (1 inch) squares.

Heat the cream, rum and vanilla in a saucepan to just below boiling point, then remove from the heat. In a bowl, beat the egg yolks and sugar together until pale then gradually add the cream, whisking all the time. Strain through a fine sieve.

Layer the bread and prunes in 4 buttered ramekins. Pour in the cream to saturate the bread. Leave to stand for about 30 minutes.

Place the ramekins in a bain-marie (or roasting tin containing enough hot water to come halfway up the sides of the ramekins). Bake in a preheated oven at 180°C (350°F) mark 4 for 35-40 minutes.

Meanwhile to make the raspberry coulis, purée the raspberries with the icing sugar and lemon and orange juices in a blender or food processor. Pass through a sieve to remove the seeds.

To make the rum sabayon, put the egg yolks, sugar and rum in a large heatproof bowl over a pan of hot water and whisk until thick and creamy. Remove from the pan and whisk until cool; then fold in the whipped cream.

To serve, turn the bread and butter puddings out of the ramekins and place on individual serving plates with a portion of the rum sabayon. Serve accompanied by the raspberry coulis.

Michael Baxter

> *"I loved the rum with the Bread and Butter Pudding."*
>
> Leslie Forbes

Caramelised Rice Pudding and Pears

with a Gingered Caramel Sauce

Rice Pudding:
115 g (4½ oz) pudding rice
600 ml (1 pint) milk
½ vanilla pod, split
115 g (4½ oz) caster sugar

Poached Pears:
4 William pears
1 vanilla pod, split
125 g (4 oz) caster sugar
15 ml (1 tbsp) lemon juice
caster sugar, for sprinkling

Custard:
4 egg yolks
15 g (½ oz) caster sugar
175 ml (6 fl oz) milk
½ vanilla pod, split

Caramel:
50 g (2 oz) caster sugar

Ginger Sauce:
2.5 cm (1 inch) piece fresh root ginger, peeled and chopped
150 g (5 oz) caster sugar
40 g (1½ oz) unsalted butter

To make the rice pudding, blanch the rice in boiling water for 2 minutes, then drain. Put the milk and vanilla pod in a heavy-based pan and bring to the boil. Add the rice and sugar, stir well and simmer for 30 minutes. Strain through a sieve.

Peel and core the pears. Put them in a pan, add water to cover, then add the vanilla pod, caster sugar and lemon juice. Bring to the boil, lower the heat and gently poach the pears for 20 minutes or until tender. Leave the pears to cool in the syrup.

Meanwhile make the custard, whisk the egg yolks with the sugar in a bowl until pale and creamy. Put the milk and vanilla pod in a saucepan and bring to the boil. Remove from the heat and allow to cool, then whisk into the egg mixture. Strain through a sieve into a bowl and stir in the rice.

To prepare the caramel, put the sugar in a small pan with 30 (2 tbsp) water over a low heat until dissolved, then boil steadily until the syrup turns golden brown. Immediately pour the caramel into the base of the pudding moulds.

Divide the rice and custard mixture between the moulds, place in a roasting tin containing enough water to come halfway up the sides of the moulds. Bake in a preheated oven at 180°C (350°F) mark 4 for 25 minutes or until set.

Meanwhile to make the ginger sauce, put the ginger and sugar in a small pan with 30 ml (2 tbsp) water. Place over a low heat until the sugar is dissolved, then cook until the syrup caramelises. Carefully add the butter and a further 75-90 ml (5-6 tbsp) water a little at a time. Heat gently, stirring, then strain.

Cut the pears into thin slices and place on a baking sheet. Sprinkle liberally with caster sugar. Put under a very hot grill to caramelise the sugar. (Alternatively you can use a blow torch.)

To serve, unmould a rice pudding on to the centre of each serving plate. Surround with the pear slices and gingered caramel sauce.

Alastair Hendy

Steamed Vanilla and Apricot Puddings

with a Fruit Coulis

40 g (1½ oz) caster sugar
300 ml (½ pint) water
225 g (8 oz) fresh apricots, stoned and chopped
1 vanilla pod

Sponge Mixture:
75 g (3 oz) self-raising flour
5 ml (1 tsp) baking powder
pinch of salt
75 g (3 oz) butter
75 g (3 oz) caster sugar
1 small egg, size 5 or 6
90-120 ml (6-8 tbsp) milk

In a saucepan, dissolve the sugar in the water over low heat. Add the chopped apricots and vanilla pod and poach for 5 minutes; discard the vanilla pod. Remove the apricots with a slotted spoon and set aside. Reduce the liquid to a syrup by fast boiling and reserve.

Put a few pieces of apricot in the base of 4 buttered dariole moulds.

To make the sponge mixture, sift the flour, baking powder and salt together. Cream the butter with the sugar until light and fluffy, then beat in the egg. Fold in half of the chopped apricots. Fold in the flour mixture with enough milk to give a soft dropping consistency.

Spoon into the dariole moulds and cover tightly with foil. Place in a saucepan, containing enough boiling water to come halfway up the sides of the moulds. Steam for 1 hour, topping up with boiling water as necessary.

Purée the remaining fruit in a food processor or blender and mix with the syrup to make the apricot coulis. Turn out the vanilla puddings onto warmed serving plates and surround with the apricot coulis.

Nancy Smith

"Big success this. The tragedy is that we always have to move along."

Leslie Thomas

Vanilla Pears

with an Almond Filling and Chocolate Sauce

175 g (6 oz) granulated sugar
juice of ½ lemon
1 vanilla pod
4 dessert pears

Almond Filling:
15 ml (1 tbsp) Grand Marnier
75 g (3 oz) white marzipan
25 g (1 oz) amaretti biscuits, crushed

Chocolate Sauce:
40 g (1½ oz) caster sugar
100 g (3½ oz) plain chocolate, chopped
20 ml (4 tsp) whipping cream
15 ml (1 tbsp) kirsch

To Decorate:
15-30 (1-2 tbsp) yogurt
25 g (1 oz) flaked almonds, toasted

Dissolve the sugar in 900 ml (1½ pints) water in a saucepan over low heat. Add the lemon juice and vanilla; bring to a simmer. Peel the pears and scoop out the cores with a melon baller, from the bases. Place the pears in the syrup. Cover with a circle of greaseproof paper and poach gently for 20-25 minutes or until tender. Leave to cool in the syrup.

To prepare the filling, work the Grand Marnier into the marzipan until smooth. Mix in the crushed amaretti biscuits.

To make the chocolate sauce, dissolve the sugar in 75 ml (5 tbsp) water in a saucepan over a low heat. Bring to the boil, then remove from the heat. Add the chocolate, stirring until dissolved, then stir in the cream and kirsch. Allow to cool.

Drain the pears and push a little filling into each one, through the base. Halve lengthwise and arrange on serving plates. Surround with chocolate sauce, dot with yogurt and feather with a skewer. Decorate with almonds.

Richard Kuch

"So beautifully made. The marzipan filling was a nice surprise."

Loyd

Left: *Vanilla Pears with an Almond Filling and Chocolate Sauce*

Leche Frita

525 ml (18 fl oz) milk
grated rind of ½ lemon
1 cinnamon stick
5 ml (1 tsp) vanilla essence
2 eggs, size 1
2 egg yolks, size 1
125 g (4 oz) granulated sugar
75 g (3 oz) plain flour
1 egg, beaten, for coating
50 g (2 oz) homemade dried breadcrumbs (see note)
corn oil, for shallow-frying
30 ml (2 tbsp) icing sugar (approximately)
2.5 ml (½ tsp) ground cinnamon

Fruit Coulis:
2 ripe mangoes
225 g (8 oz) raspberries

Put the milk in a saucepan with the lemon rind, cinnamon and vanilla. Bring slowly to the boil, remove from the heat and leave to infuse for 10 minutes.

Meanwhile in a bowl, whisk the eggs, egg yolks, sugar and flour together to a thick, smooth cream. Strain the milk through a fine sieve into the whisked egg mixture, stirring constantly. Return to the clean pan and bring to the boil, stirring constantly. Cook, stirring, for 3 minutes, until thickened and smooth.

Pour the custard into a well buttered square shallow dish of suitable dimensions to give a 2.5 cm (1 inch) depth of custard. Leave to cool for 1 hour, then refrigerate for at least 3 hours, until set firmly.

Meanwhile make the fruit coulis. Peel the mangoes and cut the flesh into chunks, discarding the stones. Put the mango flesh in a blender or food processor and work to a purée, then pass through a nylon sieve. Put the raspberries into the cleaned blender or food processor and work to a purée; sieve to remove the seeds.

Cut the firmly set custard into 5 cm (2 inch) squares. Dip each square into the beaten egg, then coat with the breadcrumbs, pressing them on firmly.

Heat a 2.5 cm (1 inch) depth of oil in a deep frying pan. Fry the coated squares in batches, turning, until browned on all sides, taking care to avoid breaking the crisp skin. Drain on kitchen paper.

Sift the icing sugar with the cinnamon then dip the leche frita in the cinnamon sugar to coat.

To serve, spoon the raspberry coulis onto one side of each serving plate and the mango coulis onto the other side. Using a chopstick, carefully feather the edges of the two sauces together. Place the leche frita in the middle and serve at once.

Derek Johns

Cook's Note

To prepare your own dried breadcrumbs put dry bread in the oven on the lowest setting until crisp, golden and well dried. Crush with a rolling pin.

Baked Bramleys

with Cobnut Stuffing and Cardamom Custard

4 even-sized British Bramley cooking apples
100 g (4 oz) cobnuts or hazelnuts
100 g (4 oz) light muscovado sugar
1 egg yolk
juice of 1 orange
150 ml (¼ pint) sweet cider
knob of butter
sugar for sprinkling

Cardamom Custard:
600 ml (1 pint) full-cream milk
50 g (2 oz) sugar
6 cardamom pods
4 egg yolks, beaten

To Serve:
apple leaves and blossom to decorate (optional)

First make the cardamom custard, combine the milk and sugar in a saucepan. Crush the cardamom pods and add to the pan. Heat the milk until it is almost boiling, cool slightly, then pour on to the egg yolks, stirring constantly.

Return to the pan and cook over a low heat, stirring continuously, until the mixture is thick enough to just coat the back of the spoon.

Cover the surface with a piece of greaseproof paper to prevent a skin forming and leave to infuse for about 1 hour.

Core the apples, retaining the stalks. Score the skin around the middle of each one.

Grind half of the nuts in a blender or food processor. Roughly chop the other half of the nuts and roast in a preheated oven at 180°C (350°F) mark 4 for about 10 minutes. Combine the ground and roasted nuts with the sugar, egg yolk and orange juice.

Stuff the apples with the nut mixture, then place in a baking dish. Pour the cider around the apples and add a knob of butter and a sprinkling of sugar. Cook in the oven for 45 minutes to 1 hour, depending on the size of the apples, basting occasionally with the juices.

To serve, strain the custard into a clean pan and reheat gently. Pop in the reserved stalks and smooth the wrinkled apple skins. Decorate each one with an apple leaf and some apple blossom if the season's right! Serve the baked apples in a pool of cardamom custard.

Linda Yewdall

Linda Yewdall – Finalist 1992

Life after MasterChef has never been busier for Linda. Most recently seen on our screens in the cookery slot on Good Morning with Anne and Nick, she has also taken the stage at the New Grand Opera House in York to give a demonstration. Linda is also contemplating buying a delicatessen to stock the best of British produce as well as doing her regular slot on York radio.

Pears Baked in a Juniper and Vanilla Sauce

50 g (2 oz) butter, unsalted
15 ml (1 tbsp) dried juniper berries (see note)
30 ml (2 tbsp) soft brown sugar
6 ripe firm pears
350 ml (12 fl oz) port
2 vanilla pods

Melt the butter in a frying pan, add the dried juniper berries and fry gently for 2-3 minutes. Add the brown sugar and allow to dissolve over a low heat.

Meanwhile peel the pears leaving the stalks on; halve and remove the cores. Place the pear halves in the pan with the juniper berries and fry gently for 5-10 minutes until slightly browned. Add half of the port and turn the pears frequently until they start to take up the port.

Using a slotted spoon, transfer the pear halves to a lightly greased baking dish. Add the remaining port to the pan with the vanilla pods and bring to the boil, then reduce the sauce by one third. Pour over the pears in the baking dish, cover with a lid and cook in the preheated oven at 180°C (350°F) mark 4 for about 1 hour until tender, basting the pears at regular intervals with the sauce.

Arrange the pears on serving plates, pour over the sauce and serve immediately, with cream.

Marc Hadley

• Cook's Note •

To improve the flavour of the dried juniper berries, soak them in gin overnight before use.

KENT STRAWBERRY KISSEL

WITH SCENTED GERANIUM MERINGUE

Kissel:

450 g (1 lb) Kent strawberries
30 ml (2 tbsp) fruit sugar
lemon juice, to taste
5 ml (1 tsp) arrowroot

Meringues:

3 egg whites
pinch of cream of tartar or salt (optional)
175 g (6 oz) geranium sugar (see below)
5 ml (1 tsp) lime or lemon juice
5 ml (1 tsp) cornflour
150 ml (¼ pint) clotted cream

To Serve:

50-75 g (2-3 oz) Alpine strawberries
4-6 tiny geranium leaves, to decorate

COOK'S NOTE

To make the geranium sugar, grind 12 freshly picked medium-sized geranium leaves of any scented, edible variety with 175 g (6 oz) caster sugar (preferably the light, raw type) in a coffee-grinder. Spread out on baking sheets and dry gently in a low oven, at 120°C (250°F) mark ½ for 10-15 minutes,until no longer moist. Store in a jar with a tight-fitting lid until needed.

To make the kissel, hull the strawberries and divide into 2 equal batches. Sprinkle the first batch with 15 ml (1 tbsp) fruit sugar and a squeeze of lemon juice. Set aside for 1-2 hours until the juices begin to seep.

Place the second batch in a stainless steel saucepan with 15 ml (1 tbsp) fruit sugar and a squeeze of lemon juice, and cook gently until completely tender. Purée (no need to sieve) and return to the saucepan. Blend the arrowroot with a little cold water, or some juice from the first batch of strawberries, then stir into the purée and bring back to the boil, stirring constantly. Once thickened, cook very gently for another couple of minutes, then allow to cool completely. Purée the first batch of strawberries, along with any syrup produced, and blend with the cooked strawberry purée. Check for sweetness, adding a little fruit sugar or lemon juice as needed, then chill until ready to serve.

For the meringues, whisk the egg whites until very stiff (a pinch of cream of tartar or salt helps). Then whisk in half the geranium sugar, whisking until completely stiff. Fold in the remaining sugar gently, along with the citrus juice and cornflour.

Spoon or pipe the meringue into 4 or 6 nests on a baking sheet lined with non-sticking baking parchment. Bake in a preheated oven, at 160°C (325°F) mark 3, for about 40 minutes, until lightly tinged with brown and surface-dry. Ease off the baking sheet and allow to cool on a wire rack.

To serve, fill each nest with a little clotted cream and Alpine strawberries. Place a geranium leaf at one edge of each meringue, and serve with a jugful of kissel.

Silvija Davidson

SUMMER FRUIT BRULÉE

450 g (1 lb) fresh or frozen summer fruits eg redcurrants, blackcurrants, raspberries and blackberries, thawed if frozen
30 ml (2 tbsp) kirsberry liqueur, kirsch or other liqueur
finely pared rind and juice of 1 small orange
5 ml (1 tsp) arrowroot or cornflour
150 ml (¼ pint) double cream
150 ml (¼ pint) natural yogurt
50 g (2 oz) dark soft brown sugar
50 g (2 oz) caster sugar

Put the summer fruit in a bowl, pour over the liqueur and leave to stand. Blanch the orange rind in boiling water for a few minutes, drain and reserve. Mix the orange juice with the arrowroot or cornflour. Strain the juice from the summer fruit and add to the arrowroot paste. Bring to the boil stirring, to thicken, then allow to cool.

Divide the fruit between 4 ramekins or other individual heatproof dishes and pour over the thickened juice. Whip the cream until it forms soft peaks. Stir the yogurt in the pot, then fold into the cream. Finely shred the blanched orange rind and fold enough into the cream to flavour to taste. Spread the cream mixture over the fruit in the small dishes and refrigerate.

Combine the sugars together and spread evenly over the cream. Preheat the grill to very hot and place the dishes underneath for a few minutes until the sugar is caramelised, then refrigerate to cool. Tap the caramel with a spoon to break it up when ready to eat.

Carol Alexander

Lavender Baked Figs on Brioche Toasts

with Cassis Glacage and Blackberry Confiture

8 fresh figs
125 g (4 oz) lavender sugar

Blackberry Confiture:
60 ml (4 tbsp) caster sugar
½ glass crème de mure, or crème de cassis
30 blackberries

Cassis Glacage:
1 egg yolk
30 ml (2 tbsp) caster sugar
150 ml (¼ pint) whipping cream
15 ml (1 tbsp) cassis purée (approximately)

To Serve:
8 slices brioche, each 1 cm (½ inch) thick

Cook's Note

Ready-made cassis purée is sold in cartons but it is not widely available. If you are unable to buy it, simply make your own blackcurrant purée.

Left: *Lavender Baked Figs on Brioche Toasts*

First make the confiture, dissolve the sugar in the liqueur in a pan over a low heat, then boil to reduce to a thick syrup. Add the blackberries and cook gently for about 2 minutes only, until softened but still retaining their shape. Remove the blackberries with a slotted spoon and set aside on a plate. Reserve the syrup.

To make the cassis glacage, whisk the egg yolk with the sugar and cream until thick, then fold in enough cassis purée to give a rich lilac colour. Set aside.

To prepare the syrup for the figs, put the lavender sugar (including flowers) and 100 ml (3½ fl oz) water in a pan over a low heat to dissolve the sugar. Increase the heat and boil to reduce the syrup slightly. Add the figs and shake the pan to coat the figs in the syrup. Transfer to an ovenproof dish, cover and place in a preheated oven at 200°C (400°F) mark 6 for 5-10 minutes to heat through. Remove from the oven and set aside.

Cut the brioche slices into rounds, then brown lightly on both sides under a hot grill.

To serve, pour or spread about a tablespoon of the glacage onto one side of an individual flameproof plate. Place under a very hot grill and watch carefully. First the egg will cook which sets the glacarge, then almost immediately the top will begin to brown. As soon as you have a nice brown topping, remove before it burns. Repeat with the other servings.

Make a cross-cut in the top of each fig and push up from the bottom so the 'petals' open out. Place a fig on each brioche toast, next to the cassis glacage and spoon over any spare syrup. Place a spoonful of blackberry confiture syrup and a pile of blackberries on each plate. Serve immediately.

Brian Tompkins

"A fabulous dessert...and so clever"

Jean Marsh

• Ingredients •

To make the lavender sugar, simply add a good handful of dried lavender flowers to a 450 g (1 lb) jar of caster sugar and leave in your storecupboard to use as you would any flavoured sugar. Lavender sugar imparts a delicious flavour to custard and makes a refreshing change from vanilla.

Raspberry and Cinnamon Torte

with Raspberry Sauce

150 g (5 oz) soft margarine
150 g (5 oz) caster sugar
150 g (5 oz) ground almonds
150 g (5 oz) self-raising flour
5 ml (1 tsp) ground cinnamon
1 egg
225 g (8 oz) raspberries

Raspberry Sauce:
225 g (8 oz) raspberries
15 ml (1 tbsp) icing sugar
5 ml (1 tsp) lemon juice

To Serve:
icing sugar and ground cinnamon, for dusting
whipped cream and Greek yogurt

Place the margarine, caster sugar, ground almonds, flour, cinnamon and egg in a bowl. Beat thoroughly to mix. Spread half of the mixture in a greased and base-lined 22 cm (8½ inch) spring-release cake tin and flatten slightly, using a fork. Sprinkle the raspberries over the mixture and dot the remaining torte mixture on top so that it almost covers the fruit.

Stand the tin on a baking sheet and bake in a preheated oven at 180°C (350°F) mark 4 for about 45 minutes, covering lightly with foil if the top is becoming too brown. When cooked, the torte will feel just firm and slightly springy. Leave in the tin to cool for about 1 hour.

Meanwhile prepare the raspberry sauce. Purée the raspberries in a food processor or blender with the icing sugar and lemon juice, then seive to remove the pips.

Turn out the cooled torte and dust with icing sugar sifted with cinnamon. Serve warm, accompanied by the raspberry sauce and cream mixed with yogurt.

Daphne Nelson

"Very, very, very, very, very good"

Loyd

Serving Suggestion

This cinnamon scented torte is particularly good served warm, with a mixture of lightly whipped cream and thick Greek yogurt.

Serpent Cake

with Oranges and Coconut Cream

Cake:
2 large sheets of filo pastry
1 egg
icing sugar, for dredging
ground cinnamon, for dusting

Filling:
225 g (8 oz) ground almonds
125 g (4 oz) icing sugar
30 ml (2 tbsp) orange flower water
15 ml (1 tbsp) water
60-90 ml (4-6 tbsp) melted butter, cooled
2.5 ml (½ tsp) almond essence
2.5 ml (½ tsp) vanilla essence
finely grated rind of ½ orange (optional)

Oranges:
2 large oranges (preferably blood oranges)
few drops of orange flower water

Coconut Cream:
25-50 g (1-2 oz) creamed coconut
150 ml (¼ pint) double cream
Cointreau, to taste

To make the cake filling, combine the ground almonds, icing sugar, orange flower water, water and cooled melted butter in a bowl. Add the almond and vanilla essences and, if desired, the finely grated orange zest. Mix well, knead to a smooth paste, then cover and chill.

Divide the chilled almond paste into 4 pieces and roll out each piece to a long sausage, 1cm (½ inch) in diameter.

Cut each sheet of filo pastry in half lengthwise. Lay out one pastry strip and place a filling 'sausage' along the bottom long edge. Roll up tightly. Repeat with the remaining filo and 'sausages'.

Line a baking sheet with non-stick baking parchment. Starting at the centre of the baking sheet, arrange the filo-covered 'sausages' in a tight spiral to resemble a coiled snake.

Brush with beaten egg and bake in a preheated oven at 180°C (350°F) mark 4 for about 10 minutes until the pastry is crisp and golden. Turn the filo cake over and bake for a further 10 minutes until the top is crisp and golden.

Transfer to a wire rack, dredge with icing sugar and decorate with fine lines of cinnamon.

Peel and carefully segment the oranges, over a bowl to catch the juice. Add a few drops of orange flower water and chill thoroughly.

Heat the coconut cream very gently until melted, adding a little water if necesary. Stir in the double cream and Cointreau to taste. Mix well; cool. The mixture may seem a bit sloppy at this stage but it will thicken on cooling.

Serve the serpent cake warm or cold. Slice and place on serving plates, with a fan of orange segments and a dollop of coconut cream.

Sue Longden

Walnut and Quince Tarts

Rich Shortcrust Pastry:
125 g (4 oz) plain flour
pinch of salt
50 g (2 oz) caster sugar
50 g (2 oz) ground almonds
75 g (3 oz) unsalted butter
juice of ½ lemon
1 egg, size 3-4

Filling:
3 eggs
50 g (2 oz) light muscovado sugar
125 g (4 oz) unsalted butter, melted
125 g (4 oz) golden syrup
finely grated rind and juice of 1 lemon
225 g (8 oz) shelled walnuts

To Glaze:
30 ml (2 tbsp) quince jelly
7.5 ml (½ tbsp) quince eau-de-vie or lemon juice

Quince Cream:
225 g (8 oz) mascarpone (Italian soft cream cheese)
25 ml (5 tsp) quince jelly
15 ml (1 tbsp) quince eau-de-vie (or to taste)

Cook's Note

Make sure you use really fresh walnuts for this tart. My local healthfood shop sells light amber walnuts, which are ideal.

To make the pastry, sift the flour and salt into the food processor bowl. Add the sugar and ground almonds and process briefly to mix. Add the butter, in pieces, and process until the mixture resembles fine breadcrumbs. Add the lemon juice and sufficient egg to bind, processing briefly until the dough begins to hold together. Gather the pastry into a ball, wrap in cling film and leave to rest in the refrigerator for 30 minutes or longer.

Roll out the pastry thinly on a lightly floured surface and use to line 4 individual 10 cm (4 inch) loose-bottomed flan tins. Line each with a disc of greaseproof paper and baking beans and bake blind at 200°C (400°F) mark 6 for 10 minutes. Remove the paper and beans and bake for a further 5 minutes.

Meanwhile prepare the filling. In a bowl, beat the eggs with the sugar, butter and syrup until smooth. Stir in the lemon rind and juice.

Divide the walnuts between the cooked pastry cases and spoon the filling mixture on top. Bake at 175°C (360°F) mark 3 for 20-25 minutes until set. Gently warm the quince jelly with the eau-de-vie or lemon juice until melted. Brush over the tarts as soon as they are removed from the oven, to glaze.

To make the quince cream, beat the mascarpone in a bowl until smooth. Gently warm the quince jelly until melted then carefully fold into the mascarpone with the eau-de-vie.

Serve the walnut and quince tarts warm, with the quince cream at room temperature.

Sue Lawrence

Pear Gratin

with Cinnamon Ice Cream

Ice Cream:

300 ml (½ pint) milk
300 ml (½ pint) double cream
1 cinnamon stick
4 egg yolks
125 g (4 oz) sugar

Gratin:

4 ripe pears
lemon juice for sprinkling
4 egg yolks
45 ml (3 tbsp) caster sugar
100 ml (3½ fl oz) double cream, whipped
125 ml (4 fl oz) Poire Williem eau-de-vie

To make the ice cream, put the milk and cream in a saucepan with the cinnamon stick and heat gently. Simmer for 5 minutes to infuse. Remove from the heat.

Beat the egg yolks and sugar thoroughly to a creamy consistency, then whisk into the milk. Remove the cinnamon stick, squeezing out the juice into the mixture. Transfer to a freezerproof container and freeze for about 2 hours, until it is the consistency of ice cream.

For the gratin, peel, core and slice the pears, then sprinkle with lemon juice to prevent browning. Arrange in 4 small gratin dishes or on heatproof plates. Beat the egg yolks and sugar together thoroughly, then fold in the whipped cream and Poire Williem. Pour the mixture over the pears, coating them completely. Bake in a preheated oven at 220°C (425°F) mark 7 for 10-15 minutes. Allow to stand for 5 minutes before serving.

Just before serving, place a scoop of cinnamon ice cream in the centre of each pear gratin. Serve at once.

Jo Eitel

Individual Apple Tarts

with Calvados flavoured Crème Chantilly

1 kg (2¼ lb) Cox's apples
15 g (½ oz) butter
1.25 ml (¼ tsp) ground cinnamon
50 g (2 oz) sugar
120 ml (4 fl oz) Calvados
225 g (8 oz) ready-made puff pastry
60 ml (4 tbsp) apricot jam

Crème Chantilly:

120 ml (4 fl oz) chilled whipping cream
25 g (1 oz) icing sugar

Set aside 4 apples. Peel, core and roughly chop the remaining apples. Place in a saucepan over a low heat with the butter. Add the cinnamon, sugar and all but 30 ml (2 tbsp) of the Calvados. Cook until the apples are soft and the mixture is reduced to a sauce, stirring occasionally. Sieve if necessary.

Roll out the pastry as thinly as possible on a lightly floured surface. Using a saucer as a guide, cut out 4 rounds, 1 cm (½ inch) larger than the saucer all round. Bend the edge of the pastry upwards to form a rim around each circle.

Spread the apple sauce over the base of the tarts. Peel, core and thinly slice the reserved apples. Arrange the apple slices over the sauce, making sure it is totally covered. Bake in a preheated oven at 230°C (450°F) mark 8 for 15 minutes. Lower the temperature to 200°C (400°F) mark 6 and bake for a further 10 minutes or until the pastry is golden brown and the apples are caramelised; make sure they do not burn.

Warm the apricot jam with 15 ml (1 tbsp) Calvaldos, then sieve and brush over the apple slices to glaze.

Prepare the crème chantilly a few minutes before serving. Whisk the cream with the icing sugar, adding the reserved 15 ml (1 tbsp) Calvados a little at a time during whisking. Take care to avoid overbeating.

Serve the apple tarts warm, with the crème chantilly.

Kieth Kheer

"*Terrific*"

Loyd

Cook's Note

For the crème chantilly, it's important to have everything well chilled, so put the bowl and whisk into the refrigerator to chill well beforehand.

***Right:** Individual Apple Tarts with Calvados-flavoured Crème Chantilly*

CHILLED ZABAGLIONE

WITH A HINT OF ORANGE

4 egg yolks
50 g (2 oz) caster sugar
150 ml (¼ pint) Marsala
30 ml (2 tbsp) Cointreau, Grand Marnier or other orange liqueur
finely pared strip of orange zest
90 ml (6 tbsp) double cream, lightly whipped

Whisk the egg yolks and sugar in a bowl until pale and frothy. Whisk in the Marsala and orange liqueur. Add the orange zest.

Place the bowl over a saucepan of simmering water and whisk the mixture, using a balloon whisk, for 10-15 minutes until thickened. Remove the bowl from the heat and cool slightly, whisking occasionally. Discard the orange zest.

Fold the cream into the slightly cooled zabaglione and pour into individual glasses. Chill before serving, with sponge biscuits.

Amita Baldock

MEDITERRANEAN ISLANDS

600 ml (1 pint) full-cream milk
1 vanilla pod
3 eggs, size 1, separated
60-75 ml (4-5 tbsp) caster sugar
15 ml (1 tbsp) rum, or orange-flavoured liqueur
125 g (4 oz) granulated sugar
25 g (1 oz) blanched almonds, chopped and toasted
fresh fruit in season, to decorate

In a large frying pan, warm the milk with the vanilla pod. To make the meringue, whisk the egg whites in a bowl until stiff, then add 45 ml (3 tbsp) caster sugar and whisk until evenly incorporated. Poach spoonfuls of the meringue mixture in the hot milk until fluffy but firm. Slide on to a large plate.

Beat the egg yolks with the remaining caster sugar. Strain in the vanilla-flavoured milk, stirring constantly. Transfer to a heavy-based pan and cook gently until the custard is thick enough to coat the back of a spoon. Add the rum or liqueur. Divide the custard between individual serving dishes and allow to cool.

To serve, float the 'islands' on the custard. Dissolve the granulated sugar in 120 ml (4 fl oz) water in a heavy-based pan over a low heat, then boil until caramelised. Stir in the toasted almonds and drizzle over the 'islands'. Decorate with small pieces of fresh fruit.

Joan Bunting

COOK'S NOTE

This is a classic French recipe and a favourite of both my mother and son. When I cook a meal as a treat, my mother always says, 'Make that thing with the meringues floating on top.'

"It's awfully good... packs a bit of a punch as well."

Loyd

Joan Bunting – Winner 1990

The inaugural holder of the MasterChef title, Joan decided to fulfil one of her lifelong ambitions and buy a house in Provence. Her guests are introduced to the food and wines of the area by Joan, who teaches cookery and leads trips to local markets. She also has a syndicated newspaper column in "The Journal" and has published a book called "Cooking with Love". Joan's plans for the future involve running workshops at her home to complement the courses held in Provence.

Right: *Mediterranean Islands*

Blackbottom Cheesecake

with Strawberries

Base:
50 g (2oz) quality dark chocolate
50 g (2oz) golden granulated sugar
15 ml (1 tbsp) strong black (espresso) coffee
dash of dark rum
50 g (2oz) unsalted butter
1 egg, size 1

Filling:
125 g (4oz) cream cheese
150 ml (¼ pint) soured cream
2 passion fruit
150 ml (¼ pint) double cream

To Finish:
250 g (8oz) ripe fragrant strawberries

Cook's Tip

This creamy exotic dessert has a very dark, sticky, fudgy chocolate base and a passion fruit flavoured cheesecake layer. Topped with 'flowers' of deep red fragrant strawberries and set off with a crescent of strawberry purée, it is irresistible. A guest at my house once proposed to this ultimate chocolate confection!

Break up the chocolate and place in a bowl over a pan of hot water, with the sugar, coffee and rum. Warm, stirring, until the chocolate has melted. Remove from the heat. Using a large whisk, beat in the butter in small pieces, a little at a time, until evenly blended. Whisk in the egg.

Butter the insides of 4 crumpet rings and stand them on a baking tray lined with non-stick baking parchment. Divide the chocolate mixture evenly between the rings and bake in a preheated oven at 150°C (300°F) mark 2 for about 40 minutes. Allow to cool, then chill.

Meanwhile make the filling. Beat the cream cheese and soured cream together in a bowl. Halve the passion fruit and scoop out the pulp and seeds into a sieve over the bowl. Press the fruit through the sieve on to the cream cheese mixture, then beat in. Add the double cream and whip until the mixture is quite stiff.

Unmould the chocolate bases on to individual serving plates. Cover with an even thick layer of filling, reserving a little for decoration. Arrange overlapping strawberry slices on top, with their pointed ends radiating out like flower petals.

Purée the remaining strawberries in a blender or food processor, then sieve to remove pips. Spoon a crescent of strawberry purée on to each plate beside the cheesecake, and pipe fine lines of cream cheese filling across it to decorate. Serve immediately.

Sarah Beattie

Raspberry Pavlovas

with a Raspberry and Sloe Gin Coulis

Pavlovas:
2 egg whites
100 g (4 oz) caster sugar

Coulis:
100 g (4 oz) sugar
finely pared rind of 1 orange
1 cinnamon stick
150 ml (¼ pint) water
150 ml (¼ pint) sloe gin
225 g (8 oz) raspberries

Syrup:
finely pared rind of 2 oranges
8 green peppercorns in brine, drained
100 g (4 oz) sugar
150 ml (¼ pint) water

To Serve:
150 ml (¼ pint) double cream, whipped
225 g (8 oz) raspberries

"Lovely sauce. Very, very good."

Jane Asher

Right: *Raspberry Pavlovas with a Raspberry and Sloe Gin Coulis*

To make the pavlovas, whisk the egg whites in a bowl until stiff, then gradually beat in the sugar, 25 g (1 oz) at a time. Spoon the meringue mixture into 8 even-sized mounds on a large baking sheet lined with non-stick baking parchment. Place in a preheated oven at 150°C (300°F) mark 2. Immediately lower the temperature to 140°C (275°F) mark 1 and bake for 1 hour, then turn off the oven, leaving the pavlovas to cool in the oven.

To make the coulis, put the sugar, orange rind and cinnamon in a saucepan with water and heat gently until the sugar has dissolved. Increase the heat, add the sloe gin and boil rapidly to reduce. Add the raspberries and leave to cool.

Discard the orange rind. Purée in a blender or food processor, then pass through a sieve to remove the pips.

To make the green peppercorn and orange syrup, cut the orange rind into strips and place in a saucepan with the peppercorns, sugar and water. Slowly bring to the boil, then simmer until reduced to a syrupy consistency.

Spread a pool of raspberry coulis on each serving plate and place a meringue on the coulis. Cover the meringue with whipped cream and raspberries. Pour over some of the orange syrup. Place a second meringue on top of the raspberries, setting it at an angle. Decorate the coulis with a splash of cream, feathered with a skewer. Serve immediately.

Joy Skipper

Blueberry Shortcake

with a Fruit Coulis

Blueberry Cream:
200 g (7 oz) blueberries
300 ml (½ pint) whipping cream
50 g (2 oz) icing sugar, sifted

Fruit Coulis:
50 g (2 oz) blueberries
50 g (2 oz) raspberries
30 ml (2 tbsp) icing sugar, sifted
15 ml (1 tbsp) drambuie

Shortbread Biscuits:
175 g (6 oz) plain flour
25 g (1 oz) caster sugar
75 g (3 oz) butter
30 ml (2 tbsp) milk

To Decorate:
icing sugar, for dusting
a little single cream
few raspberries and blueberries

To make the blueberry cream, place the blueberries in a food processor and work to a purée, then sieve to remove the seeds. Put the whipping cream in the food processor and process until it forms firm peaks; do not overwork. Turn into a bowl and fold in the icing sugar and blueberry purée until evenly blended. Cover and place in the refrigerator to chill and 'firm up' the mixture.

To make the fruit coulis, purée the blueberries and raspberries in

the food processor and pass through a sieve twice to remove all the seeds. Add the icing sugar and drambuie and stir until the sugar has dissolved and the coulis has a smooth consistency. Cover and chill in the refrigerator until required.

To make the shortbread biscuits, sift the flour into the processor and add the sugar, butter and milk. Process briefly until the mixture forms a smooth dough; the mixture must not be too 'short' otherwise it will crumble when rolled out thinly.

Roll out the dough very thinly on a floured surface. Using a 6 cm (2½ inch) pastry cutter, cut out 12 biscuits. Place on a lightly greased baking tray and bake in the top of a preheated oven at 180°C (350°F) mark 4 for 8-10 minutes or until crisp and golden. Remove from the oven and carefully transfer to a wire rack to cool.

To assemble the shortcakes, place a biscuit in the centre of each serving plate. Spoon on some of the blueberry cream, then cover with another biscuit. Add another spoonful of blueberry cream and finally top with a biscuit. Sprinkle with icing sugar. Pour some of the fruit coulis around each shortcake to make a pool. Spoon tiny blobs of single cream on to the coulis and draw a cocktail stick through the cream to make a feathered design. Top with a few raspberries and blueberries.

Betsy Anderson

Left: *Blueberry Shortcake with a Fruit Coulis*

Chocolate Gâteau

6 eggs, size 3, separated
100 g (3½ oz) caster sugar
100 g (3½ oz) ground almonds
100 g (3½ oz) plain dark chocolate, grated

Topping:
100 g (3½ oz) plain dark chocolate, in pieces
300 ml (½ pint) whipping cream

Chocolate Caraque:
100 g (3½ oz) plain dark chocolate, in pieces

"*Exquisite!*"

Loyd

Grease a 20 cm (8 inch) loose-bottomed cake tin and line with greaseproof paper.

In a bowl, whisk the egg whites until they form firm peaks. Whisk in the sugar, 15 ml (1 tbsp) at a time. In another bowl, lightly beat the egg yolks, then gently fold into the whisked mixture. Add the ground almonds and grated chocolate and fold in lightly until evenly incorporated. Turn the mixture into the prepared cake tin and bake in a preheated oven at 170°C (325°F) mark 3 for 45 minutes. Allow to cool in the tin before turning out.

To make the chocolate caraque, melt the chocolate in a heatproof bowl over a pan of hot water, then spread in a thin layer on a marble slab or board. When the chocolate is just set, scrape off long curls by pushing a large knife across the surface of the chocolate.

To prepare the topping, melt the chocolate in a heatproof bowl over a pan of hot water. Remove the bowl from the heat and leave to cool slightly. In a bowl, whip the cream until it holds its shape, then fold in the cooled melted chocolate until evenly incorporated.

Spread the chocolate cream evenly over the top and sides of the cake. Decorate with the chocolate caraque.

Tony Davis

Caramelised Orange and Chocolate Mousse Gâteau

225 g (8 oz) plain chocolate
100 g (4 oz) unsalted butter
3 eggs, lightly beaten

Candied Orange Zest:
3 oranges
200 ml (7 fl oz) sugar syrup

Chocolate Glaze:
150 ml (¼ pint) double cream
175 g (6 oz) plain chocolate, finely chopped

To Decorate:
caramelised orange segments (optional)

"If you knew that was coming you probably would not eat for a few days! That is just wonderful."

Loyd

Wrap the outside of a 15 cm (6 inch) springform cake tin in a double layer of foil to prevent seepage. Butter the cake tin and line the base with a round of non-stick baking parchment. Butter the paper.

To prepare the candied orange zest, finely pare long strips of zest from the oranges, using a potato peeler. Set aside one third for decoration; coarsley chop the rest. Blanch the strips of zest in boiling water for 8-10 minutes, then refresh under cold water; repeat with the chopped zest. Simmer the strips of zest in the sugar syrup for 3 minutes, then remove with a slotted spoon. Repeat with the chopped zest.

Combine the chocolate and butter in a large heatproof bowl over a pan of hot water. Let stand, stirring occasionally, until the chocolate is melted and smooth.

Put the eggs in a large mixing bowl set over a pan of simmering water and stir constantly until warm to the touch. Remove from the heat. With an electric mixer, beat the eggs until they triple in volume and form soft peaks when the beater is lifted.

Fold half the whisked eggs into the melted chocolate until partially incorporated. Add the remaining eggs and fold in just until they are evenly blended and no streaks remain. Fold in the chopped candied orange zest.

Pour at once into the prepared cake tin and smooth the surface with a spatula. Place in a larger roasting pan and add enough hot water to the pan to reach about two thirds of the way up the side of the cake tin.

Bake in a preheated oven at 220°C (425°F) mark 7 for 5 minutes. Cover the top of the cake tin with foil and bake for a further 10 minutes. Remove the cake tin from the roasting pan and let cool on a wire rack for 45 minutes. Then cover and refrigerate until chilled and very firm.

To make the chocolate glaze, in a small heavy-based saucepan, scald the cream. Remove from the heat and immediately add the chocolate. Stir gently until the chocolate is melted and smooth.

To unmould the cake, use a small spatula or a blunt-edged knife around the edge and remove the side of the cake tin. Carefully invert the cake onto a plate and remove the bottom of the tin. Peel off the baking parchment. Pour the tepid chocolate glaze on to the centre of the cake, letting it cascade over the side. Allow to set. Decorate the cake with the candied orange zest, and caramelised orange segments, if desired.

Caramelised orange segments: Peel and segment an orange, discarding all pith. Place on a foil-lined tray and sprinkle with sugar. Caramelise under a preheated hot grill.

Martha Spencer

Cook's Note

This sumptuous rich gâteau serves 6-8. I have found that Lindt chocolate gives the best result.

Right: *Caramelised Orange and Chocolate Mousse Gâteau*

White Chocolate Mousse

with Strawberries

100 g ($3\frac{1}{2}$ oz) bar white chocolate
40 g ($1\frac{1}{2}$ oz) butter
$1\frac{1}{2}$ egg yolks
5 egg whites
30-45 ml (2-3 tbsp) whipping cream

Shortbread:
50 g (2 oz) butter
25 g (1 oz) caster sugar
125 g (4 oz) plain flour

To Serve:
125 g (4 oz) strawberries
8-10 lychees
75 ml (5 tbsp) Amaretto di Saronno liqueur

Melt the chocolate with the butter in a bain-marie (or heatproof bowl over a pan of simmering water). Take off the heat and stir in the egg yolks. Whisk the egg whites until stiff and fold into the chocolate mixture, a spoonful at a time. Whip the cream until soft peaks form, then fold into the mousse. Leave to set.

To make the shortbread, cream the butter and sugar together until light and fluffy. Using your fingers, work in the flour to a soft dough. Be careful not to make it too short or the shortbread will crumble. Lightly roll out to a 5 mm ($\frac{1}{4}$ inch) thickness and cut out rounds, or any shape you like. Place on a lightly greased baking sheet and bake in a preheated oven at 180°C (350°C) mark 4 for 10-15 minutes until golden. Cool on a wire rack.

Meanwhile, soak the fruit in the liqueur for 20 minutes or longer, depending on how alcoholic you wish it to be! Drain.

Divide the fruit between individual glasses. Top with the chocolate mousse and decorate with the shortbread to serve.

Melanie Jappy

Behind the Scenes...

"Ken Russell was among our most exuberant and unconventional judges. Teamed up with the great Irish cook – Darina Allen – he couldn't resist asking her for a good soda bread recipe. Darina responded immediately. Whilst our contestants were furiously cooking away, Ken and Darina were up to their arms in flour backstage as a quick lesson in baking took place."

...Loyd

Dark Chocolate Leaves

layered with White Chocolate Mousse in a pool of Vanilla Sauce

White Chocolate Mousse:
1 gelatine leaf
240 g ($8\frac{1}{4}$ oz) white chocolate
2 egg yolks
200 ml (7 fl oz) double cream, lightly whipped

Crème Anglaise:
250 ml (8 fl oz) milk
3 egg yolks
45 ml (3 tbsp) vanilla sugar

Chocolate Leaves:
125 g (4 oz) best-quality dark chocolate

Chocolate Sauce:
45 ml (3 tbsp) milk
50 g (2 oz) dark chocolate, grated

To Decorate:
8 Cape gooseberries

To make the white chocolate mousse, soak the gelatine in a little cold water until soft. Meanwhile, grate the white chocolate into a bowl. Squeeze the excess water from the gelatine, then carefully melt it in 30 ml (2 tbsp) water. Pour the melted gelatine on to the chocolate and stir over a bowl of hot water until it has melted. Allow to cool, but not set. Mix the egg yolks into the cooled chocolate, then fold in the lightly whipped cream. Transfer to a suitable shallow rectangular dish and refrigerate until needed.

To make the crème anglaise, pour the milk into a saucepan and slowly bring to a simmer over a medium heat. In a bowl, whisk the egg yolks and vanilla sugar together until light and thick. Gradually whisk in half of the hot milk, then add to the remaining milk in the saucepan and mix well. Cook over a medium heat, stirring constantly, until the sauce thickens slightly. Do not allow to boil. Pour into a clean bowl and allow to cool.

To make the chocolate leaves, dampen a baking sheet with water and line it with non-stick baking parchment. Melt the chocolate in a bowl over a pan of hot water, then spread very thinly on the lined baking sheet. Allow to set, then cut into 4 cm ($1\frac{1}{2}$ inch) squares or shapes as desired.

To make the chocolate sauce for feathering, place the milk in a saucepan. Add the chocolate and bring to the boil, stirring constantly until the chocolate has melted and the sauce is smooth and shiny.

To serve, spoon the vanilla sauce on to serving plates and feather with the chocolate sauce. Layer the chocolate leaves with white mousse, then arrange in the centre of each plate. Peel back the papery skins from the Cape gooseberries and use to decorate the dessert. Serve immediately.

Vanessa Binns

Below: *Dark Chocolate Leaves Layered with White Chocolate Mousse*

Amaretti Chocolate Tortes

4 amaretti biscuits
250 g (9 oz) plain dark chocolate
30 ml (2 tbsp) liquid glucose or glycerine
30 ml (2 tbsp) Amaretto di Saronno liqueur
300 ml (½ pint) double cream
12-16 blanched almonds
150 ml (¼ pint) single cream
knob of butter

Line the bases of 4 ramekin dishes with circles of greaseproof paper. Crush the amaretti biscuits finely and divide evenly between the ramekins.

Break 8 oz (225 g) of the chocolate into small pieces and put into a heatproof bowl with the liquid glucose or glycerine and liqueur. Place the bowl over a saucepan of hot water until the chocolate is melted and smooth. Remove the bowl from the pan and leave to cool slightly.

Whip the double cream until just thickened, then stir 30 ml (2 tbsp) into the chocolate mixture. Add this chocolate mixture to the remaining cream and stir until well blended. Pour the mixture into the ramekins, dividing it evenly, and tap the ramekins to level the surface of the mixture. Chill in the refrigerator for at least 45 minutes to set firmly.

Meanwhile melt the remaining chocolate. Dip each almond into the chocolate to half coat, and place on a foil-lined plate to set. Reserve the remaining chocolate.

To serve, re-melt the reserved chocolate and stir in the butter. Spoon into a small greaseproof paper piping bag fitted with a very fine plain nozzle. Run a knife around each ramekin. Place an inverted plate centrally over each ramekin and invert the dish and plate. Carefully remove the ramekins and greaseproof paper.

Pour a little cream around each torte, pipe lines of chocolate on the cream and feather with the point of a skewer. Decorate the tortes with the half-coated almonds.

Patti Hall

"This is what a chocolate dessert should be."

David Burke

Bitter Chocolate Marquise

with Cloudberry Sauce

200 g (7 oz) quality bitter chocolate (Valrhona)
15 ml (1 tbsp) strong black coffee
30-45 ml (2-3 tbsp) cloudberry liqueur, or framboise eau-de-vie
125 g (4 oz) unsalted butter, softened
125 g (4 oz) caster sugar
30 ml (2 tbsp) cocoa powder
3 egg yolks
300 ml (½ pint) double cream

Cloudberry Sauce:
450 g (1 lb) cloudberries (see note)
15 ml (1 tbsp) cloudberry liqueur, or framboise eau-de-vie
125-175 g (4-6 oz) caster sugar, to taste

To Decorate:
handful of cloudberries

Cook's Note

I usually serve this irresistible rich dessert with a raspberry sauce – made from flavourful Scottish raspberries. If you are lucky enough to find cloudberries, do use them; otherwise raspberries make a perfectly good substitute.

Break the chocolate into a heatproof bowl and add the coffee and liqueur. Place over a pan of hot water until melted. Allow to cool.

In a bowl, beat the butter with half of the sugar until light and fluffy. Fold in the cocoa powder. In another bowl, whisk the egg yolks with the remaining sugar until pale. Lightly whip the cream.

Beat the cooled chocolate into the butter and cocoa mixture, then stir into the beaten egg yolk mixture. Lightly fold in the cream.

Line 4 small ramekins with cling film. Pour in the chocolate mixture and tap the ramekins to level. Cover and chill for 1½ -2 hours until set.

Meanwhile, prepare the cloudberry sauce. Purée the cloudberries with the liqueur and sugar to taste in a blender or food processor. Sieve to remove all the pips.

To serve, invert the marquise on to individual plates, covered with a pool of cloudberry sauce. Cut out a tiny wedge of each marquise to reveal the texture. Decorate with a few fresh cloudberries.

Sue Lawrence

Rhubarb and Elderflower Syllabub

with Shortbread Hearts

6 stalks rhubarb
60 ml (2 fl oz) elderflower wine
50 g (2 oz) caster sugar
5 ml (1 tsp) ground ginger
10 ml (2 tsp) arrowroot

Syllabub:
300 ml (½ pint) double cream
90 ml (6 tbsp) elderflower wine
squeeze of lemon juice
50 g (2 oz) caster sugar
5 ml (1 tsp) brandy

Shortbread:
50 g (2 oz) butter
50 g (2 oz) caster sugar
few drops of vanilla essence
50 g (2 oz) plain flour
25 g (1 oz) self-raising flour
icing sugar, for dusting

Cut the rhubarb into 2.5 cm (1 inch) pieces and place in a heavy-based saucepan with the wine, sugar and ginger. Bring to the boil, lower the heat and simmer until tender. Mix the arrowroot with a little cold water until smooth, then stir into the rhubarb mixture. Heat, stirring, until slightly thickened. Allow to cool.

Spoon the rhubarb into the base of 4 tall glasses, reserving 45 ml (3 tbsp) of the mixture for the syllabub.

To make the syllabub, whip the cream until thick, then whisk in the wine, lemon juice, sugar and brandy. Stir in the reserved rhubarb mixture and spoon in to the glasses. Chill until required.

To make the shortbread, cream the butter with the sugar and vanilla essence. Stir in the plain and self-raising flours. Shape into a ball and leave to rest for 30 minutes. Roll out thinly and cut out heart shapes, using a suitable cutter. Bake in a preheated oven at 180°C (350°F) mark 4 for 10 minutes until pale golden. Immediately transfer to a wire rack and dust with icing sugar. Allow to cool.

Serve the syllabub dessert with the shortbread hearts.

Sarah Giles

Blackberry and Cassis Fool

450 g (1 lb) blackberries
175 g (6 oz) sugar
60 ml (4 tbsp) water
60 ml (4 tbsp) crème de cassis
300 ml (½ pint) double cream, chilled
icing sugar, for dusting

Set aside 4 good blackberries for decoration.

Put the rest of the blackberries in a saucepan with the sugar and water. Cover and cook gently for 20 minutes or until the fruit is pulpy. Leave to cool for 10 minutes, then sieve to remove the blackberry pips.

Pour the cassis into 4 individual glasses or a large serving bowl and chill.

Whip the cream until stiff peaks form, then fold in the blackberry purée until evenly combined. Carefully spoon the mixture into the serving glasses or bowl, keeping the cassis at the bottom. Chill for at least 1 hour.

Decorate with the reserved fruit and dust with icing sugar. Serve with almond pastry twists.

Tricia Humber

"*That would go down in a hurry, I promise you.*"

David Gower

Sparkling Melon and Lime Soup

with Lacy Tuiles

1 ripe Galia or Charentais melon
finely pared rind and juice of 2 dark green limes
25 g (1 oz) sugar
90 ml (6 tbsp) Champagne or sparkling wine

Lacy Tuiles:
75 g (3 oz) butter, softened
75 g (3 oz) caster sugar
50 g (2 oz) plain flour
pinch of salt

To Decorate:
strawberries
mint sprigs

First make the lacy tuiles, in a bowl, beat the butter and sugar together until light and fluffy. Stir in the flour and salt.

Place teaspoonfuls of the mixture on a greased baking tray, spacing them well apart. Flatten with the back of a spoon. Bake in a preheated oven at 200°C (400°F) mark 6 for 5-6 minutes until golden brown.

Remove from the oven and while still hot, curl over a small rolling pin. Leave until firm, then carefully remove and place on a wire rack to cool completely.

Halve the melon and scoop out 350 g (12 oz) flesh, reserving the juice. Squeeze out extra juice from the melon to yield 150 ml (¼ pint); if necessary make up to this quantity with water. Pour the melon juice into a saucepan. Add the pared lime rind and sugar. Bring to the boil and boil for 2-3 minutes.

Allow to cool, then strain into a blender or food processor. Add the melon flesh and lime juice and work to a purée. Divide between individual serving bowls and chill before serving.

Just before serving, carefully add the Champagne or sparkling wine and decorate with strawberries and mint sprigs. Serve with lacy tuiles.

Shirley Faulkner

"*Pretty good fun – more of a cocktail than a pudding*"

Loyd

Right: *Sparkling Melon and Lime Soup with Lacy Tuiles*

SPICED AMBER CUPS

WITH ORANGE BOUCHÉES

Amber Cups:
10 ml (2 tsp) powdered gelatine
150 ml (¼ pint) orange juice (some ideally from blood oranges)
250 ml (8 fl oz) Moscatel de Valencia
4-5 young rosemary sprigs
generous grating of nutmeg
finely grated rind of ½ orange

Orange Bouchées:
1 egg
40 g (1½ oz) soft margarine
50 g (2 oz) caster sugar (preferably golden)
2.5 ml (½ tsp) finely grated orange rind
25 g (1 oz) ground almonds
25 g (1 oz) self-raising flour

To Finish:
30 ml (2 tbsp) whipped cream
2.5 ml (½ tsp) caster sugar
dash of Amaretto di Saronno liqueur, or almond essence

"If grown-ups eat jelly, this is what they eat. I must have the recipe. It's absolutely delicious."

Raymond Blanc

For the amber cups, soften the gelatine in 45 ml (3 tbsp) orange juice, then place the bowl over a pan of simmering water until completely dissolved. Add to the remaining orange juice with the wine. Strip the leaves from the rosemary and crush using a pestle and mortar. Add to the orange mixture with the nutmeg. Check the flavouring and strain through a muslin-lined sieve. Add a little grated orange rind.

Divide the jelly mixture between 4 small glasses, filling them about two-thirds full. Refrigerate for 2 hours.

To make the orange bouchées, whisk together the egg, margarine and caster sugar. Add the grated orange rind and ground almonds, then fold in the flour. Divide between very well-oiled mini bun tins. Bake in a preheated oven at 200°C (400°F) mark 6, for about 8 minutes.

Before serving, mix the whipped cream with the caster sugar and almond liqueur (or essence), and top each glass with a teaspoonful of sweetened cream. Serve the amber cups with the orange bouchées.

Alison Riddel

LEMON AND LAVENDER SORBET

3 lemons
175 g (6 oz) sugar
300 ml (½ pint) water
6 drops of Culpeper's lavender water
1 egg white

To Decorate:
shredded lemon zest
lavender flowers and leaves (optional)

Thinly pare the rinds from two of the lemons and place in a saucepan with the sugar and water. Heat gently until the sugar is dissolved, then simmer for 5 minutes. Remove the lemon rind and allow to cool.

Squeeze the juice from all 3 lemons and add to the syrup with the lavender water. Transfer to a suitable container and freeze, stirring occasionally. When the mixture is half-frozen, whisk to break down the ice crystals. Whisk the egg white until stiff, then fold into the half-frozen sorbet. Freeze, stirring occasionally, until the sorbet resembles firm snow.

Serve scooped into glass dishes, decorated with lemon zest, lavender flowers and leaves if available.

Linda Yewdall

• COOK'S NOTE •

Once it reaches the correct consistency this sorbet can be left in the freezer until required, but it is at its best served the day it is made.

Right: *Lemon and Lavender Sorbet*

Provençal Lavender Honey and Ginger Ice Cream

in Brandy Snap Baskets

Ice Cream:
4 egg yolks
25 g (1 oz) caster sugar
300 ml (½ pint) single cream
6 pieces preserved stem ginger in syrup, finely chopped
15 ml (1 tbsp) ginger syrup (from the stem ginger jar)
30 ml (2 tbsp) provençal lavender honey
300 ml (½ pint) double cream

Brandy Snap Baskets:
25 g (1 oz) butter
30 ml (2 tbsp) granulated sugar
15 ml (1 tbsp) golden syrup
30 ml (2 tbsp) plain flour
2.5 ml (½ tsp) ground ginger
pinch of salt
12 ml (½ tbsp) brandy
12 ml (½ tbsp) lemon juice

Chocolate Sauce:
125 g (4 oz) dark chocolate, in pieces
75 ml (2½ fl oz) milk
15 ml (1 tbsp) double cream
15 g (½ oz) caster sugar
15 g (½ oz) butter

Raspberry Coulis:
125 g (4 oz) fresh or frozen raspberries
lemon juice, to taste
icing sugar, to taste

To make the ice cream, whisk the egg yolks and sugar together in a bowl until pale and creamy. Heat the cream until almost boiling, then pour on to the egg mixture, stirring. Strain back into the pan and cook very gently, stirring constantly, until the custard thickens slightly, just enough to coat the back of a spoon. Remove from the heat and stir in the chopped ginger, ginger syrup and honey. Allow to cool.

Whip the double cream lightly and stir into the cold custard. Place in an ice-cream maker and freeze for approximately 40 minutes. Turn into a freezerproof container and place in the freezer.

To make the brandy snap baskets, melt the butter, sugar and syrup together in a small pan over a low heat. Remove from the heat and beat in the rest of the ingredients.

Cook's Note

Using an ice-cream maker gives this ice cream a very light texture. If you do not own one, whisk the ice cream 2 or 3 times during freezing to break down the ice crystals.

Place teaspoonfuls of the mixture on a baking sheet lined with non-stick baking parchment, spreading the mixture into even-sized circles, and leaving plenty of space between them for spreading. Bake in a preheated oven at 180°C (350°F) mark 4 for 6-8 minutes until golden brown.

Let cool for 20 seconds only, then drape each brandy snap over an upturned greased ramekin dish, moulding the sides firmly to make a basket. Allow to cool, then remove.

To make the chocolate sauce, melt the chocolate in a bowl over a pan of hot water. In a small pan, gently heat the milk, cream and sugar together, then bring to the boil, stirring. Pour over the melted chocolate, then return to the pan. Bring to the boil and simmer for 15 seconds. Remove from the heat and whisk in the butter.

Transfer the ice cream to the refrigerator about 15 minutes before serving to soften.

To make the coulis, purée the raspberries in a blender or food processor with a little water if necessary. Pass through a sieve and flavour with a little lemon juice or icing sugar as required.

Serve the ice cream scooped into brandy snap baskets, with the raspberry coulis and warm or cold chocolate sauce.

Anne Heaton

Halva and Rosewater Ice Cream

with Walnut Cake and Quince Syrup

Walnut Cake:

50 g (2 oz) unsalted butter, softened
100 g (4 oz) walnuts, finely chopped
5 ml (1 tsp) baking powder
15 ml (1 tbsp) plain flour
100 g (4 oz) caster sugar
1 egg white, size 3
2 egg whites, size 4

Halva and Rosewater Ice Cream:

3 large eggs
50 g (2 oz) caster sugar
5 ml (1 tsp) rosewater
300 ml (½ pint) whipping cream
100 g (4 oz) halva

Quince Syrup:

50 g (2 oz) caster sugar
1 quince, peeled and chopped
2 green cardamoms

Butter an 18 cm (7 inch) spring-form cake tin and line the base with greaseproof paper.

In a bowl, beat the butter with the chopped walnuts, baking powder, flour and 75 g (3 oz) of the sugar until evenly mixed. Add the size 3 egg white and mix again.

In another bowl, whisk the two size 4 egg whites until stiff, then gradually sprinkle in the remaining 25 g (1 oz) sugar, whisking the time. Carefully fold the two mixtures together and spoon into the prepared tin. Level the surface.

Bake in a preheated oven at 180°C (350°F) mark 4 for 20 minutes or until a knife inserted in the middle of the cake comes out clean. Allow to cool a little before releasing the cake from the tin.

To make the ice cream, in a bowl, whisk the eggs, sugar and rosewater together until the mixture is pale and thick enough to leave a ribbon trail when the whisk is lifted.

In another bowl, whip the cream until it forms soft peaks, then crumble in the halva. Lightly fold into the whisked egg mixture. Turn into a freezerproof container and freeze until firm.

To make the quince syrup, dissolve the sugar in 900 ml (1½ pints) water in a heavy-based pan over a low heat. Bring to the boil and simmer for 15 minutes. Add the quince and cardamoms and simmer, uncovered, for approximately 1½ hours or until the syrup turns a rich amber colour. Press through a sieve, discarding the fruit. If the syrup is too thin, reduce by boiling to about 200 ml (7 fl oz). Cool before serving.

Remove the ice cream from the freezer a few minutes before serving and soften at room temperature. Serve the ice cream on a pool of quince syrup, surrounded by thin slices of walnut cake.

Marwan Badran

Tart Orange and Lemon Ice Cream

with a Bitter Chocolate Sauce

Ice Cream:
4 small mineolas, or other small oranges
2 eggs, separated
75 g (3 oz) caster sugar
finely grated rind and juice of 2 lemons
finely grated rind of 2 oranges
300 ml (½ pint) double cream
juice of 1 lime

Bitter Chocolate Sauce:
200 g (7 oz) bitter chocolate
30 ml (2 tbsp) brandy or Cointreau
60 ml (4 tbsp) double cream
1 small coffee-cup strong black coffee (espresso)

To Decorate:
60 ml (4 tbsp) single cream
shredded lemon zest, blanched
16 raspberries

To prepare the mineolas or oranges, slice off their tops and trim their bases to a flat surface. Scoop out as much flesh and pith as possible, then place the orange shells in the freezer.

"That's spectacular."

Glenys Kinnock

Whisk the egg yolks with the caster sugar until pale and thick. Add the grated lemon and orange rinds. In another bowl, whip the cream until thick, then slowly add the lime juice and nearly all of the lemon juice.

Whisk the egg white until soft peaks form. Fold the whipped cream into the egg yolk mixture, then carefully fold in the egg white. Transfer to a freezerproof container and place in the freezer for 30 minutes.

Transfer to an ice-cream maker and churn for 15 minutes. Alternatively, whisk by hand. Spoon the ice cream into the mineola or orange shells and place in the freezer until firm.

To make the bitter chocolate sauce, combine the chocolate, brandy or Cointreau, cream and half of the coffee in a heavy-based saucepan. Stir over a moderate heat until smooth. Cool, then adjust the consistency as necessary by adding more (cooled) coffee. Leave in the refrigerator until required.

To assemble, pour out a little pool of chocolate sauce on to each serving plate and carefully position the ice cream filled oranges in the centre. Spoon 4 drops of cream on the plate (at 12, 3, 6, and 9 o'clock), streak with the tip of a knife, then mount each with a raspberry. Sprinkle with lemon zest to serve.

Adrian Bregazzi

"It's brilliant, brilliant."

Rick Stein

ICED GINGER BOMBES

WITH VANILLA STARS

2 egg whites
100 g (4 oz) caster sugar

To Assemble:
250 ml (8 fl oz) double cream
grated rind of 1 lemon
30 ml (2 tbsp) kirsch
15 ml (1 tbsp) caster sugar
45 ml (3 tbsp) marinated ginger and crystallised fruits (see note)

Vanilla Stars:
100 g (4 oz) unsalted butter, chilled
50 g (2 oz) icing sugar
75 g (3 oz) plain flour
25 g (1 oz) cornflour
pinch of baking powder
pinch of salt
1 moist vanilla pod, seeds and pulp extracted

To Serve:
few preserved stem ginger slices
kirsch for sprinkling

COOK'S NOTE

These are very pretty frozen in individual bombe moulds but, if you don't have any, use a shallow cake tin instead. To save time, you could use ready-made meringues – very lightly toasted. You will need 65 g (2½ oz).

To make the meringues, whisk the egg whites until stiff, then gradually whisk in half of the sugar a spoonful at a time. Fold in the rest of the sugar, using a metal spoon, to yield a firm, glossy meringue. Spoon into small mounds on a baking sheet lined with non-stick baking parchment. Bake in a preheated oven at 95°C (200°F) barely mark ¼ for 2 hours. Transfer to a wire rack to cool.

"Good balance. Absolutely wonderful."

Sue Lawley

Line 4 individual bombe moulds with cling film. Break up the meringues roughly. Whisk the cream until fairly stiff, then fold in the meringues together with the remaining ingredients. Divide between the moulds; freeze until firm.

VANILLA STARS

These vanilla biscuits melt in the mouth, but also under the rolling pin, so handle the dough very carefully! You may find it easier to roll it between sheets of lightly floured non-stick baking parchment. The above quantities will make about 15 stars.

To make the vanilla stars, cream the butter with the icing sugar in a food processor. Sift the dry ingredients together and add to the creamed mixture with the vanilla pulp and seeds. Work briefly, until the dough begins to hold together. Chill in the refrigerator for about 30 minutes.

Carefully roll out the dough to 5 mm (¼ inch) thickness. Cut out stars, using a suitable cutter, prick with a fork and place on a baking sheet. Bake in a preheated oven at 180°C (350°F) mark 4 for 15-20 minutes until pale golden brown. Cool on a wire rack.

Turn the iced bombes out on to plates and top with a little ginger and kirsch. Serve with the vanilla stars.

Orlando Murrin

• INGREDIENTS •

I keep a jar of sliced preserved stem ginger, crystallised pineapple and sultanas macerating in brandy in my refrigerator. Chopped up, they add a luxurious touch to desserts.

ICED COFFEE AMARETTI SOUFFLÉS

12 amaretti biscuits
2 egg whites
175 g (6 oz) vanilla sugar (see note)
90 ml (6 tbsp) water
7.5 ml (1½ tsp) instant coffee dissolved in 7.5 ml (1½ tsp) hot water, or very strong black coffee
15 ml (1 tbsp) Grand Marnier
350 ml (12 fl oz) double cream

To Serve:
4 toasted whole almonds
icing sugar for dusting

Prepare 4 ramekins by securing a non-stick baking parchment collar around each one, to stand 5 cm (2 inches) above the rims. Put the amaretti biscuits in a plastic bag and crush with a rolling pin.

Whisk the egg whites until stiff. Dissolve the sugar in the water in a heavy-based saucepan over a gentle heat, then bring to the boil and bubble for 3 minutes. Pour the syrup onto the egg whites in a thin stream, whisking constantly at a high speed. Continue whisking until cool, then add the coffee and Grand Marnier. Whip the cream in a separate bowl until thick but not stiff, then lightly fold into the mixture.

Spoon the soufflé mixture into the ramekins until they are just over half-full, then sprinkle on a thick layer of crushed biscuits. Cover with the remaining soufflé mixture, until it stands 2.5 cm (1 inch) above the rims.

Freeze the soufflés for 1½-2 hours, then carefully remove the paper collars. Coat the sides and tops with the remaining crushed biscuits and place a toasted almond on the top of each one. Dust the tops with sifted icing sugar.

Sarah Marsh

"That is yummy."

Loyd

COOK'S NOTE

Leave a vanilla pod in a jar of caster sugar to impart flavour.

Behind the Scenes...

"What happens to all the food? I'm afraid that we judges rarely get second helpings even though every contestant cooks enough for four. As the judges "deliberate, cogitate and digest" the studio crew attack our competitors' cooking with increasingly knowledgable gusto. Leftovers may be non-existent, but we have the best fed crew in television."

...Loyd

Right: *Iced Coffee Amaretti Soufflés*

INDEX